D0862935

Climate Change, Trade and Modes of Production in Sub-Saharan Africa

STUDIES IN THE AFRICAN PAST 3

Series editors:

Felix Chami
Gilbert Pwiti
&
Chantal Radimilahy

DAR ES SALAAM UNIVERSITY PRESS LTD.

Published in Tanzania by:

Dar es Salaam University Press Ltd
University of Dar es Salaam
P.O. Box 35182
Dar es Salaam, Tanzania
w.w.w.dup.co.tz

© Felix Chami, Gilbert Pwiti & Chantal Radimilahy, 2003

ISBN   9976 60 392 4

All rights reserved. No part of this publication may be reproduced, stored in a retrieval system or transcribed in any form or by any means, electronic, mechanical, photocopying, recording or otherwise without the prior written permission of Dar es Salaam University Press Ltd.

Contents

iv

List Tables, Figures/Maps and Plates

vi

Figures

Plates

Preface

This is the third volume of the book series Studies in the African Past. The series was launched in 2001 with the publication of scientific reports of the eastern and southern Africa archaeology project called "Human Responses and Contributions to Environmental Change." The second volume was also published under the auspices of the same project in 2002.

This volume is being published by another phase of the same project, now called "African Archaeology Program." The editors, members of the project, invited papers from colleagues in the project from countries such as Madagascar, Mozambique, Zimbabwe, Botswana, Namibia, Tanzania, Kenya, Uganda, Nigeria and Mali. However, the book series is open to all scholars interested in the African past from all over the world.

This volume has been called "Climate, Trade and Modes of Production in Sub-Saharan Africa." There are three papers that have focused on climate namely the chapters by Felix Chami, Munyaradzi Manyanga and Lorraine Swan. The first paper demonstrates how archaeology can be used to show past climatic changes and the human responses to it. The coast of East Africa has been shown to have a sequence of climate changes comparable with other regions of Africa. Manyanga's paper is about the cultural continuity in the Shashi-Limpopo but with the same bias towards climatic/environmental change. Swan's paper shows how either iron technology or climate change or both could be studied to assist in the understanding of cultural change in the past.

Some papers are research reports of particular sites to demonstrate cultural sequence/continuity and other aspects such as pottery, resource utilisation and rock art. Kwekason and Chami's excavations of rock shelters in the Lake Nyanza area is one such examples. John Kinahan's excavation of a rock shelter in Namibia is another example. The paper by Leon studies pottery of central Madagascar showing different cultural groups and their mobility. One paper, that of Edward Matenga, focuses on how the people of Great Zimbabwe exploited various plant resources.

Some papers have focused on the evolution of culture and trade. Pikirayi's is such an example showing how trade in the Indian Ocean affected the Mutapa Culture of Zimbabwe between AD 1500-1800. The paper by Rasoarifetra also reflects on how the Indian Ocean trade network affected cultural activities in Madagascar in the second millennium AD. A paper by Fulorunso addresses the question of gender in Archaeology drawing on ethno-archaeological examples from the Tiv people of Nigeria.

F. Chami, G. Pwiti and C. Radimilahy, 2003

CONTRIBUTORS

Caleb Fuloronso is Reader and Head of Department of Anthropology and Archaeology, Ibadan University, Nigeria.

Felix Chami is an Associate Professor, University of Dar-es-Salaam, Tanzania

John Kinahan works with the Namibia Archaeological Trust

Amandus Kwekason is Senior Archaeologist, Dar-es-Salaam National Museum, Tanzania

Edward Matenga is Director, Great Zimbabwe Monuments.

Munyaradzi Manyanga is a Lecturer, University of Botswana

Innocent Pikirayi is a Senior Lecturer, University of Zimbabwe

Bako Rasoarifera works with University Museum, Madagascar

Darot Rasolofomampianiani Leon works with the University Museum, Madagascar

Lorraine Swan is Principal Curator of Archaeology, the National Museums and Monuments of Zimbabwe.

Enquiries about the book series should be sent to:

Prof. Felix A. Chami
University of Dar es Salaam
P O Box 35050
Dar es Salaam, Tanzania

Email: fchami@udsm.ac.tz

OR

Prof. Gilbert Pwiti
University of Zimbabwe
Faculty of Arts
P O Box MP167
Harare, Zimbabwe

Email: gpwiti@arts.ac.tz

OR

Prof. Chantal Radimilahy
University Museum
BP. 564-Antananarivo
Madagascar
E-mail: chradimi@syfed.refer.mg

Book orders should be submitted to:

Dar-es-Salaam University Press Ltd.
University of Dar-es-Salaam,
P O Box 35182,
Dar-es-Salaam,
Tanzania.

Studies in the African Past Book Series

(Editors)

Vol.1   People, Contacts and the Environment in the African Past (2001).

Vol. 2   Southern Africa and the Swahili World (2002)

Vol. 3   Climate, Cultural Change and Modes of Production (2003)

Climatic Change on the Coast of East Africa Since 3000 BC: Archaeological Indicators

Felix A. Chami

This work is concerned with climate change that took place over the coast of East Africa for the last five thousand years beginning from about 3000 BC. Data for this time period for the rest of the region of eastern and southern Africa has been collected and discussed by different scholars. Bryson and Bryson (1997) and Hassan (1997a) have examined the general African trend in the Holocene. Robertshaw and Taylor (2000) have specifically examined the Great Lakes Region. Butzer *et al* (1972), Livingstone (1975), and Hamilton (1982) have discussed the Rift Valley and the Great Lakes Region. Bell (1970) and Hassan (1981) report about the Nile valley. Deacon and Deacon (1999), Tyson and Lindesay (1992) and Huffman (1996) have written on southern Africa and Maley (1993) on the equatorial region. Using archaeology, palynology, geology and more recent historical sources, a climatic record spanning many thousands of years has been established. Bryson and Bryson (1997) have used what they have called "macrophysical climatic modelling" method.

The definition of what is climate has been discussed by various scholars including Lamb (1972) and Bryson and Bryson (1997). It suffices here to use Lamb's (1972:5) definition of climate as "the sum total of the weather experienced at a place in the course of the year over the years.

As far as I am aware, no climatic data has until now been reported from

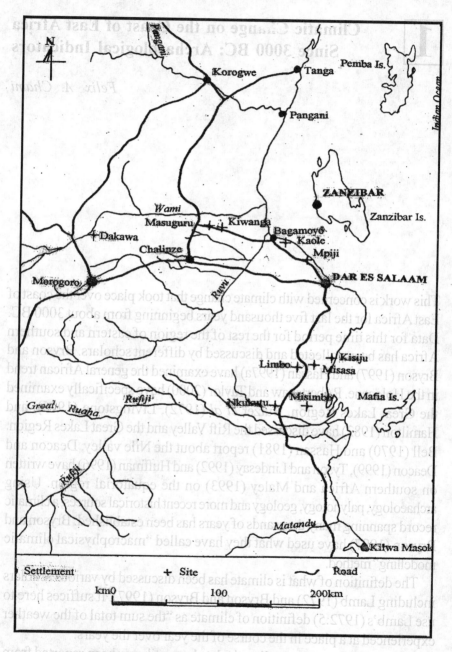

Figure 1.1: *Map showing the East African coast study area*

the coast and the islands of East Africa. Such a study could have contributed comparative data to be used to improve the understanding of climatic change in the African past. The whole discussion about past African climatic change presumes that the Western Indian Ocean Seaboard shared all the climatic vicissitudes experienced by the interior of Africa. Whereas this could be true for most periods it is good to use available data to evince this correlation. The aim of this work is therefore to discuss the data now available, mostly from archaeological evidence, to outline periods of climatic change on the coast of East Africa (Figure 1.1).

THE PROBLEM

It was noted at the outset that the past pattern of climatic change has already been established only that no data had hitherto been collected from the coast of East Africa to enrich the pattern already established. Whereas a sequence of climate change had been reported to about 3000 BC (Hamilton 1982; Butzer *et al* 1972), the time after that till now has been described by most scholars as dry (Butzer et al 1972: 1074; Livingstone 1975; Maley 1993). The situation is seen to have been even drier after 2000 BC. According to Livingstone (1975: 273), the past thousand years "have been dry over a wide area, but the effects of drought on the vegetation are compounded by the influence of agricultural and pastoral people". Indeed when Sutton (1977) discussed the effects of climatic change for the Holocene cultural period for the region extending from Sahara to East Africa this is what he had to conclude:

By the second millennium BC drier conditions again set in, and a climatic regime was established which has remained relatively stable till now (Sutton 1977: 32).

The study of the records in Egypt from about the 7th century AD has shown that despite the accepted stable drier period covering the last four thousand years one could still show some climatic variations which affected ecological systems. Hassan's (1981: 1143; see also 1997a & b) data of the Nile flood discharge, which is determined by rainfall in East Africa and Ethiopia, is shown in Table 1.1.

Table 1.1: *Interpretation of Hassan's (1981) cumulative curves of the Nile flood discharge.*

AD	CLIMATIC RECORD
1700-1850	high discharge/wetter
1500-1700	data missing
1250-1400	low discharge/drier
1100-1250	high discharge/wetter
950-1100	low discharge/drier
850-950	high discharge/wetter
600-850	low discharge/drier

Tyson and Lindesay (1992) have compiled data for southern Africa as shown in Table 1.2. Huffman (1996) obtained the picture in Table 1.3 after reviewing Tyson and Lindesay's (1992) contribution. How would data from the coast of East Africa stand in relation to a theory of relative dryness in the last 5000 years and in relation to what is already established for the Nile Valley and southern Africa?

Table 1.2: *Climate change for southern Africa according to Tyson and Lindesay (1992)*

AD	CLIMATIC RECORD
1790-1810	wetter
1675-1780	drier
1500-1675	wetter
1300-1500	drier
900-1300	wetter
600-900	drier
250-600	wetter
100-200	drier

Table 1.3: *Huffman's (1996) refinement of Tyson and Lindesay's climatic sequence*

AD	CLIMATIC RECORD	CAL. AD
1790-1810	warm/wet	same
1675-1780	cool	same
1500-1675	warm/wet	1425-1675
1300-1500	cool/dry	1290-1425
900-1300	Warm/wet	900-1290
600-900	cool	No data
250-600	warm/wet	500-700
100-200	cool	No data

CLIMATIC RECORD FROM THE COAST OF TANZANIA

A discussion of archaeological sites dating from about 3000 BC found on the coast and islands of Tanzania since 1987 has been offered elsewhere (for conspectus see Chami 1998, Chami 2001a and Chami 2001c). The location of some sites, cultural sequences and soil profiles shed light on the question of climatic change. The location of archaeological sites comprises open air sites located on the hills and valley bottoms and those found in coral (limestone) caves and coral islands. The cultural sequence ranges from Late Stone Age (LSA), through the Early Iron Working (EIW) period, to those of the recent centuries. Whereas soil profiles on the hill sites do not show much colour change over time, those from the valleys and caves do so showing different climatic periods.

Machaga Cave: Zanzibar

The limestone cave was found to have several cultural layers comprising LSA with levels dating back to 2847-2568 and 813-791 BC, the Triangular Incised Ware (TIW) tradition with known dates of AD 600-900 and the Neck Punctated (NP) or Swahili tradition dating between AD 1250-1500 (see Table 4). Whereas the LSA tradition was found in two natural layers together measuring 80cm, which suggests a long occupation period, the later traditions, which belong to the Iron Working period, were found compressed in a layer measuring 50cm. As an indicator of climatic change, the LSA layer was separated from TIW tradition by a layer with lime suggesting a long time period of water seepage from the roof. Another more pronounced lime layer was found to separate the TIW and the NP cultural traditions.

Missing from the cave cultural sequence included the EIW tradition dated in many parts of the coast of East Africa from between 100 BC - AD 600, the Plain Ware (PW) tradition found on the Tanzanian coast dating between AD 900-1250 and the Post Swahili (PS) traditions dating after AD1500. It would seem that the lime layers stood in the place of the EIW and PW traditions suggesting that the cave was too wet for occupation during those periods. Continuous dripping of water in the cave would have made it wet and containing more lime. It should be noted that it is the constant seepage of water through weak points which create stalagmites and stalactites in limestone caves.

It would seem therefore that it was not possible to occupy the cave during the EIW and NP periods because the climate was wetter. The cave would have been damp and the water table would have been higher. The occupation would have resumed when the climate was drier and the cave would have been the only source of water. Today the cave of Machaga is the only place nearby where one finds fresh water during the dry season after all the wells dug in the village becoming saline.

Ukunju Cave, Juani, Mafia Island

Excavations at the Ukunju cave sites, now in the process of being reported, found below 80cm to about 200cm a cultural layer belonging to an aceramic LSA tradition. It was observed that the LSA materials recovered below 120cm were in a wet condition and the water table was reached at about 160cm.

Excavations also recovered two potsherds of the EIW tradition in the layers above 80cm. The two potsherds of the EIW tradition are however insignificant because the open sites of the island of Juani, where the cave is located, are littered with potsherds of the EIW tradition. It could still be safe to argue that the people of the EIW tradition did not settle in the cave although they could have visited it for water in the dry season.

Other traditions, like the LSA, found to have abundant cultural materials in the Juani cave, include the NP/Swahili tradition (AD 1250-1500) and a PS tradition (AD 1650-1800). Missing from the cave is the TIW tradition (AD 600-900), which has not been found anywhere on the islands of Mafia, and that of the PW which is widespread on the open sites of the islands of Mafia.

It can be argued, therefore, that the climate was dry during the time of the LSA occupation because the larger part of the LSA cultural horizon is found within the modern water table. It must have been drier than it is today for the occupation to have taken place. During the EIW period the climate must have been very wet to the extent that the large open sites, discussed below, occurred in many parts of the islands of Mafia (see Chami 1999a). The worst dry climate must have occurred in the time of the TIW tradition when not only the caves of Mafia were avoided, but the Mafia archipelago was completely abandoned probably because there was no water. This is also probably the time when the islands were coined "Mafia" meaning the "land of death" ('ma' is land and 'fia' is die).

The islands of Mafia were reoccupied in the time of the PW tradition when the climate was wet again and the people of the NP traditions survived when the climate was drier by building lime reservoirs or resorting to settling in caves where they could get water. The presence in the cave of the PS tradition of AD 1650-1800 would also suggest that this time period was drier compared with the earlier PS period of AD 1500-1650.

Open Sites of Mafia

The open sites of the Mafia Archipelago provide further good data for climatic change. It should be noted that the larger island lacks reliable streams of water to sustain a population during the dry climate. This is why the ancient population, including the EIW people, concentrated on the southwestern part where today there are four streams flowing semi-annually. It is also in the southwestern part where there are good agricultural soils. The adjacent coral islands of Chole and Juani have some good soil for cultivation, but with no permanent fresh water. Under a dry climate the water table gets depleted or becomes salty.

The largest population which ever lived on the islands of Mafia, as seen from the archaeological record (see Chami 1999a), is that of the EIW tradition of the first five centuries AD. The three phases of the EIW tradition, Limbo, Kwale and Mwangia (see Chami 1998) are represented in these islands. The population seems to have been larger in the third century AD in the Kwale period (see dates in Table 1.4). What should be noted here is that the climate must have been wetter than that of today because even the small island of Jibondo, which is mainly coral with no soil for cultivation and no underground water was settled in the EIW period. The community, which had lived in Jibondo since a few centuries ago, had used lime/cement rainwater reservoirs. It also seems that the population of the EIW tradition that lived on the other island such as Juani would have been larger than that living there today. The EIW people occupied other small coral islands without a permanent source of water including Koma and Kwale.

Other traditions which seem to have been established on the open sites of the islands of Mafia suggesting a wetter climate include PW, whose sites are found in some areas superimposing those of the EIW traditions. Sites with such superimposition include Mlongo in Mafia, Juani, Jibondo and Kwale (Chami 1999a). The PW tradition is also found in the northern part of Mafia. It has been noted earlier that the traditions that succeeded the PW tradition could settle on the islands even when the climate was drier because lime was used since then to make reservoirs which collected rainwater.

The Rufiji Region Sites

Surveys on the northern hills of the Rufiji Delta have found many sites of different cultural periods (see Chami 2001a). Two sites with LSA cultural horizons have been found with their cultural materials mixed with those of EIW at the lower levels of the occupation. It would suggest that it was the same people who changed their culture by adopting a new incoming EIW cultural package including iron smelting and bevelled and fluted pottery. Apart from microlithic tools, pottery with wider comb stamping like that of the Rift Valley Narosura tradition is found (see Odner 1972; Chami 2001a). Other objects of the LSA tradition found include grooved sand stones and fragments of stone bowls.

The dates for the LSA in the Rufiji are still unknown. A charcoal sample collected from the site of Kibiti (Mkukutu) from a context dominated by the LSA cultural materials offered a date of the third century AD. It is apparent that this is the date for the EIW tradition.

There were many people of the EIW tradition on the hills north of the Rufiji River extending to the town of Kimansichana 60 km to the north. The soils on which they lived are red where they probably cultivated sorghum and millet. As with Mafia, the three phases of EIW tradition are represented, but the population seems to have been larger during the Mwangia phase dating between AD 400-600.

The concentration of the EIW sites on the hills and their absence in the valleys suggests that the climate was wet. The valleys would constantly have been flooded and the water table would have been high. The occupation of the hills also suggests that there was enough rainfall for cultivation of millet and sorghum. With the swelling of rivers and lakes irrigation was probably attempted (see Chami 2001a).

Also dominant on the hills are sites of the PW tradition, some like that of Limbo found superimposed on the layers of the EIW traditions. Sites of PS are also found on the hills.

On the contrary, most sites of the people of the TIW tradition, except those that seem to have inherited an ancestral EIW site like Kibiti, are found in the valley bottoms and lake margins where it would have been impossible to settle today. One site of this nature is the one found in a valley with a stream of water before crossing to Mchukwi if coming from Kibiti. Pottery of the TIW tradition associated with daub fragments is found scattered along the stream. The present conditions do not allow a sizable settlement of the valley because it gets flooded during the rainy season. Under wetter climatic periods it would have been impossible even for a few houses to be located in the valley.

Another site is that of Itonga valley, less than a kilometre east of the town of Bungu. Here, right in the valley inundated by the modern flood discharge is found a culturally rich TIW site about 60 cm below the surface. The site was discovered because modern villagers living on the elevated landscape dug waterwells in the valley to suffice during the dry season. The water table is found at 60cm or below depending on the harshness of the dry season. It is apparent that the people of the TIW period, between AD 600-900, must have settled in the valley when the climate was very much drier compared with today and when there were no heavy rains to flood their valley settlement. Moreover, the water table was lower than that of today probably by a metre.

More incontrovertible evidence which suggests that the people of the TIW tradition lived in the dry period is that of Misasa, an archaeological site located about 6 kilometres from the ocean opposite Kisiju (see Fig.1.1). Here, at the margin of the lake, between 40-80 cm below the surface, is found a culturally rich site with more remains of trade goods found than in any other TIW site on the coast of Tanzania apart from Kilwa and Unguju Ukuu. As is shown in Figures 1.2 and 1.3, a site lying below 40 cm of the modern surface near the lake margin would have been inundated by the modern swelling of the lake even during the dry season. The TIW tradition has dates ranging from AD 600-900 (Table 1.4).

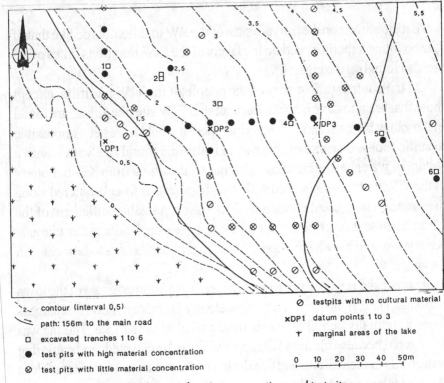

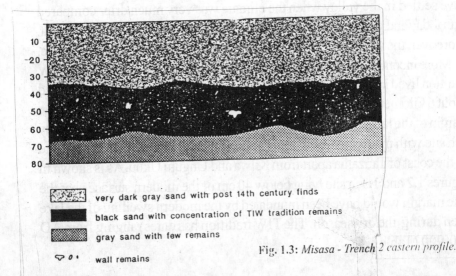

Fig. 1.2: *Misasa - elevations, excavations and test pits*

⌓ testpits with no cultural material

✕DP1 datum points 1 to 3

⅄ marginal areas of the lake

0 10 20 30 40 50m

〜2〜 contour (interval 0,5)

⌐ path: 156m to the main road

□ excavated trenches 1 to 6

● test pits with high material concentration

⊗ test pits with little material concentration

▨ very dark gray sand with post 14th century finds

▮ black sand with concentration of TIW tradition remains

▧ gray sand with few remains

▽ 0 ٠ wall remains

Fig. 1.3: *Misasa - Trench 2 eastern profile.*

Table 1.4: *C14 dates for sites of different traditions from the coast of Tanzania*

Cultural Period	Site	Lab. No.	C14 Date (calib)
NP/Swahili	Kaole	Pta-8303	AD 1202-1274
		Pta-8302	AD 1397-1427
PW	Changwehela	Ua-2089	AD 1042-1221
TIW	Kaole	Ua-2093	AD 781-884
		Ua-2092	AD 667-801
	Misasa	Ua-2595	AD 659-775
		Ua-2597	AD 536-639
EIW	Kivinja	Ua-10932	AD 431-637
	Mlongo/Mafia	Ua-12714	AD 233-406
	Kwale Island	Ua-10287	AD 425-561
		Ua-10286	AD 241-409
	Kibiti	Ua-11774-11776	AD 230-570
	Limbo	Beta-24626	90 BC-AD 74
		Beta-24624	167 BC-AD 69
LSA	Machaga/Zanzibar	GrA-14155	813-791 BC
		GrA-14158	2847-2568 BC

Also found at the site of Misasa is the NP/Swahili tradition with Islamic pottery dating between AD 1300 -1500. Missing at the site of Misasa are the EIW and the PW traditions which, as noted earlier, are found spread over some elevated landscapes. This surely suggests that in the time period of those two missing traditions it was difficult to live near the modern lake shore because of a wetter climate.

At Kivinja along the old sea-shore line, at a point where a stream of water enters the ocean, are found several sites. On the higher platform away from the stream are found sites of EIW, PW and a PS tradition. The PS tradition should date between AD 1500 and 1650 as it has the earliest European beads. Near the stream, in the area flooded by the modern rainy season, are found potsherds of the TIW tradition. This again suggests that the TIW tradition lived in the area when the stream was dry or was only seasonal.

Dietary Evidence

This line of inquiry in relation to climatic change is yet to be accorded the attention it requires in East Africa. Observations from archaeological sites so far indicate that the people of LSA tradition consumed a lot of shellfish and land snails (Gastropod). Data from Machaga cave suggests that land snails constituted the main diet of the LSA people. Similar data is obtained from the caves in Mafia although there the shellfish, mainly conch (*Strombus alatus*), and the land snails seem to have been consumed equally. The exploitation of shellfish went hand in hand with the hunting of a variety of other animals while the Zanzibar rock hyrax (*Procavia capensis*), an animal no longer found in the islands, seems to have dominated the menu of the wild animals.

The coming of the EIW tradition changed the food pattern. So far, only a few animal bones and shells have been recovered from the EIW sites on the coast and islands. A current argument that the red/brown acidic soils on which the sites are located may have caused rapid decay of animal and plant remains does not get support from the EIW sites found on sandy soils and coral areas on the islands of Mafia and Kwale. While the argument surely accounts for the partial disappearance of the animal and plant remains, it would seem that hunting and fishing were not the main activities of the EIW people, but cultivation and iron smelting.

Abundant remains of shells and bones of wild animals reappear in the period of the TIW tradition from about AD 600 to 900. Most sites or cultural horizons of the TIW tradition like those of Machaga cave, Mpiji and Kaole are found to have middens of bones and shells of animals, both marine and terrestrial. Such hunting and fishing activities disappeared again in the PW period to emerge again in the NP/Swahili time period. At this latter period, sites like those of Kaole, Zanzibar and Kanga north of Mafia are found to have large quantities of shellfish and Gastropod remains.

The same pattern is observed from sites in southern Africa. For instance Chibuene, a TIW site also with a 12-15th century occupation, has mounds of marine shells of the same time periods (Sinclair 1987: 86-87: Sinclair *et al.* 1993). Another example comes from Natal cave sites where a cultural sequence beginning from the LSA period bears layers of marine shell remains. In Natal, a major shift in food pattern took place after 2000 BP after herders and domesticated livestock arrived with pottery. Then "shellfish were collected on a smaller scale than during the megamidden period. Protein came largely from non-marine resources"(Deacon and Deacon 1999:152).

In relation to the above food data, the environment data comes from the fact that marine shell collections have been found to be an activity conducted by various communities during a time of stress. According to Msemwa (1994: 311) shellfish exploitation is a strategy to minimise risks due to poor agricultural yields caused by draught or shortage of the preferable food resources. It is also during a time of stress when agricultural people subsidise their diet with hunted wild animals. Wetter climates are also not good for shellfish growth because the river outlets and mangrove forests become less saline and hence there is a decline in shellfish exploitation (Msemwa-*pers comm*).The association of the LSA, TIW and NP traditions with large accumulations of remains of marine and terrestrial animals would suggest that those time periods were difficult times due to dry climate.

DISCUSSION

The presentation of climatic data from different parts of Africa has shown that the climate was generally drier after 3000 BC. Opinion generated from such a conclusion is that there has not occurred a major climatic impact worth studying since then because "a climatic regime was established which has remained relatively stable till now" (Sutton 1977: 32).

Table 1.5: *Derived climate record from archaeological sites from the coast and islands of Tanzania*

Cultural Tradition	Date Range	Derived Climate Record
Post Swahili-phase 2	AD 1650-1800	drier
Post Swahili-phase 1	AD 1500-1650	wetter
Neck Punctating/Swahili	AD 1250-1500	drier
Plain Ware	AD 900-1250	wetter
Triangular Incised Ware	AD 600-900	drier
Early Iron Working	100 BC- AD 600	wetter
Late Stone Age	3000 –100 BC	Drier (data fragmentary)

It has been shown that within the relatively stable climate which ensued after 3000 BC, and more so after 2000 BC, fluctuations have occurred which disrupted life and caused communities settled in one area for a long time to move to other appropriate localities. Some of the climatic fluctuations have been preserved in the Egyptian records (Bell 1970; Hassan 1981) and established by other studies from South Africa (Tyson and Lindesay 1992; Huffman 1996) and now from the coast of Tanzania.

The picture established for the period 3000 BC to about BC/AD changeover is however vague. It has been shown that the Egyptian data between 2000 BC to the beginning of the first millennium AD is fragmentary. The South African data is more available for the period after BC/AD changeover and what is available before that time period is said not to fit the rest of the African climatic pattern (Deacon and Deacon 1999:21). For the coast of East Africa only a few archaeological sites are known for the period before BC/AD changeover. However, the formation of stalactites and stalagmites in some archaeological limestone caves should provide a better picture for future work.

It has been shown, however, that the excavations of two limestone caves on the islands dating between 3000 BC to the last century BC show that the caves could have been occupied for a long time period. It was noted earlier that wetter climates are not good for limestone cave occupation. The finds in the caves of a long time of occupation, although there could have been minor climatic fluctuations in between, would suggest that at least the last two thousand years BC were generally drier.

It was shown above that more rich data exists for the period after BC/AD changeover. The archaeology of the coast of East Africa suggests a wetter climate for the first six hundred years AD. This time period of EIW has sites located on the hills with red/brown soils where it was possible to grow sorghum and millet. Comparable data from southern Africa, according to Tyson and Lindesay (1992), suggests that the dates of AD 100-200 had been cool or drier and only the time period AD 200-600 fits into the wetter East African climate pattern. However, Huffman (1996: 56) has omitted the period AD 100-200 from the pattern for lack of data. He has also calibrated the period AD 200-600 to obtain dates of AD 500-700 suggesting that this was the wetter period in southern Africa.

Contrary to Huffman's (1996) revision, the archaeology of southern Africa does not show any hiatus for the period AD100-200. Archaeological reports from southern Mozambique and in the eastern parts of South Africa contain data from sites of the EIW tradition dating back to the early centuries AD and identified as Matola or the East African Kwale variant (Klapwijk 1974; Cruz e Silva 1980; Sinclair et al 1993:417). The sites which are reported here to occur on the elevated landscapes with arable soils and iron ore are also reported to have occurred during the wetter climate (see Whitelaw and Moon 1996). It would seem that the drier climate in southern Africa ensued after about AD 600 as the population started concentrating near the marshlands and river valleys and as it happened on the East African coast populations near the ocean started to exploit more marine resources, i.e. mussels (*see* Whitelaw and Moon 1996).

Probably a more controversial aspect is Huffman's (1996) revision of Tyson's and Lindesay's (1992) dates of AD 200-600 to AD 500-700. This revision, which sees the wetter climate moving up to AD 500-700, does not concur with the data from the coast of East Africa and southern Africa as shown above. Furthermore, data from other parts of southern Africa suggests that AD 600-900 was drier. Recent studies from Zimbabwe suggest that the 7th and 8th centuries AD sites of Kadzi (Pwiti 1996: 133) were located in the valleys near the river banks. The burials of that time period are now in danger of erosion by the modern flood discharge (Pwiti 2002). This suggests that the Kadzi people must have occupied the sites when it was quite dry with less danger of floods.

It would be interesting to find out what happened in Madagascar and Comoros in the first millennium AD as so far no archeological sites are known dating before 9th century AD. However, the debate about how the Madagascan *hippopotamus* and related water animals became extinct in about the second part of the first millennium AD is another very interesting matter which needs to be explored in relation to climate change. *Hippopotamus* populations would need a good amount of water to cool off in and also grass for food. In the case of the climate getting dryer, as we have seen between AD 600 and 900, it is likely such animals would have been adversely affected and any other factor like human predation would assist in their depletion. The argument put forward for their extinction is blitzkrieg, suggesting that anthropogenic factors led to the depletion of the animals (see MacPhee and Burney 1991).

The Nile records as presented by Hassan (1981) which mostly reflect the climate in eastern Africa agree with the finds from the coast of East Africa and from southern Africa as presented by Tyson and Lindesay (1992). AD 600-900 was a drier period for eastern and southern Africa. Indeed archaeologists working in the Great Lakes Region have found the period between 600 and 900 difficult to study because of dearth of data. This observation suggests that there was a catastrophe that depopulated the region. According to Schmidt (1997: 18-19) the population dwindled from about AD 600, first in the interior, away from the lake margin, and then in the rest of the region. This episode continued until about 900-1000 when the new population using pottery decorated with roulettes settled in.

> We do not have any direct evidence for disease or widespread epidemics. The increasing population of pastoralism - perhaps linked to more grasslands resulting in deforestation - undoubtedly contributed to the movement north into open grasslands...(Schmidt 1997:19).

It is now very convincing that the episode being explained by Schmidt above relates to a harsh, drier climate the effects of which on the Tanzanian coast and islands and on the Nile Valley have been discussed. The eastern and southern African records suggest that from AD 900 to AD1300 it was generally a wetter period. The East African coastal data also agrees with the rest that there was a drier period from about AD 1300 to about 1500, followed by a wetter period between AD 1500-1650 and from about AD 1800 followed by a drier period (Robertshaw and Taylor 2000).

The climatic pattern for the coast of East Africa for the EIW and slightly earlier also has support from some ancient literature. For instance, when Pliny substantiated the cinnamon route, alleged to have gone through the coast of East Africa, he suggested that the eastern Africans, who had been passing the spices to the northerners, were living in caves. It was shown earlier that cave occupations took place on the coast and islands of Tanzania before the early EIW period or the BC/AD changeover and also thereafter between AD 600-900. The two periods were of drier climates. The report about cinnamon originating from East Africa and associated with caves appeared at the time of the Greeks between 300 BC to about the end of the first century BC which agrees with our archaeological evidence.

Furthermore, the author of *Periplus*, writing in the first century AD, reported an East African island he called Menuthias, which was about 30 km from the mainland which "was wooded and has rivers" (Casson 1989:5). As Menuthias Island is today thought to be Zanzibar (see Casson 1989; Chami 1999b), which although wooded does not have streams large enough to be viewed as rivers, it would suggest that East Africa was very wet during the time of the Periplus in the first century AD.

Another important contribution comes from Cosmas Indicopleustes who wrote in about AD 547. Discussing about a trade activity which was going on between Ethiopia (Axum) and a gold bearing country of East Africa which was located south of the Equator and near the ocean, Cosmas reported that the region was quite wet:

In going they marched very slowly, chiefly because of the cattle, but in returning they quickened their pace lest on the way they should be overtaken by winter and its rains. For the sources of the river Nile lie somewhere in these parts, and in winter, on account of the heavy rains, the numerous rivers which they generate obstruct the path of the traveller...during the three months the rain falls in torrents, and makes a multitude of rivers (Freeman-Grenville 1975: 7).

CONCLUSION

The purpose of this work was to show that climate change took place on the coast of East Africa in the last 5000 years and these fluctuations affected human settlement. Another purpose was to compare the pattern observed in the archaeology with that observed elsewhere in the rest of Africa from the Nile Valley to southern Africa. Climate studies in the rest of Africa used methods such as palynology, historical records and some geological formations. My attempt in this paper was to present data emanating from archaeological observations. The results show that the observed pattern of climate change do substantially agree with the pattern derived from other traditional methods. Archaeological observations could be used, like dendrochronology has been used to C14, to check the climate patterns developed using other non-archaeological methods.

It was shown that while data for the last three millennia BC may need to be subjected to further studies in relation to climate change on the coast of

East Africa, archaeology shows that the EIW communities of the first five centuries AD experienced a wetter climate. This situation forced them to settle on hills and elevated landscapes cultivating soils which were then arable. It was during the people of TIW, living between AD 600 and 900 that the climate became extremely dry to the extent that those who survived the catastrophe moved to other landscapes with lakes, rivers or water tables. It has been hypothesized that coral islands with no stable water sources like Mafia were abandoned. The same has been observed for the Great Lakes Region. Various climatic flunctions occurred after AD 900, the easily observed one being the drier climate of the time of the 13th century which lasted for about two centuries. This is the time of the rise of the Swahili culture when coral and lime started being used to build water reservoirs and to build deep water wells like that of Kilwa with underground tunnels to fetch the water.

REFERENCES

Bell, B. (1970)
   "The Oldest Records of the Nile Floods." *The Geographical Journal* 135 (4):569-573.
Bryson, R. and Bryson, R. (1997)
   "Macrophysical Climatic Modelling of Africa's Late Quaternary Climate: Site-specific, High-resolution Applications for Archaeology." *African Archaeological Review* 14(3): 143-160.
Butzer, K. *et al.* (1972)
   "Radiaocarbon Dating of East African Lake Leves." *Science* 175 (4027): 1069-1076.
Casson, L. (1989)
   Periplus Maris Erythraei. Princeton: University Press.
Chami, F. (1994)
   "The Tanzanian Coast in the First Millennium AD." *Studies in the African Archaeology* 7. Uppsala: Societas Archaeologica Upsaliensis.
Chami, F. (1998)
   "A Review of the Swahili Archaeology." *African Archaeological Review* 15(3): 199-221.
Chami, F. (1999a)
   "The Early Iron Age on Mafia and its Relationship with the Mainland." *Azania* 34:1-10.
Chami, F. (1999b)
   "Roman Beads from the Rufiji Delta, Tanzania. First Incontrovertible Link with Periplus." *Current Anthropology* 40(2): 237-241.
Chami, F. (2001a)
   "The Archaeology of the Rufiji Region." In Chami, F., Pwiti, G. and Radimilahy, C. (eds.), *People, Contacts and the Environment in the African Past*. Studies in the African Past 1: 7-20. Dar-es-Salaam: University Press Ltd.

Chami, F. (2001b)
"Chicken Bones from Neolithic Limestone Cave Site, Zanzibar." In Chami, F., Pwiti, G. and Radimilahy, C. (eds), *Peoples, Contacts and the Environment in the African Past*, 84-97. Studies in the African Past 1. Dar-es-Salaam: University of Dar-es-Salaam Press Ltd.

Chami, F. (2001c)
"People and Contacts in the Ancient Western Indian Ocean Seaboard or Azania." *Man and Environment* (special theme on the Indian Ocean in Antiquity) (2) 27 (1): 33-44.

Cruz e Silver, T. (1980)
"First Indications of Early Iron Age in Southern Mozambique: Matola IV 1/68." In Leakey, R and Ogot, B. (eds.), *Proceedings of the 8ᵗʰ Panafrican Congress of Prehistory and Quaternary Studies*, Nairobi 1977: 349-350. Nairobi: The International Louis Leakey Memorial Institute for African Prehistory.

Deacon, H. J. and Deacon, J. (1999)
Human Beginnings in South Africa. Cape Town: David Philip Publishers.

Freeman-Grenville, G. (1975)
The East African Coast: Selected Documents From the First to the Earlier Nineteenth Century. Oxford: Clarendon Press.

Hamilton, A.C. (1982)
Environmental History of East Africa. London: Academic Press.

Hassan, F. (1981)
"Historical Nile Floods and Their Implications for Climatic Change." *Science* 212: 1142-1145.

Hassan, F. (1997a)
"The Dynamics of a Riverine Civilisation: a Geoarchaeological Perspective on the Nile Valley, Egypt." *World Archaeology* 29 (1): 51-74.

Hassan, F. (1977b)
"Holocene Paleoclimates of Africa." *African Archaeological Review* 14(4): 213-230.

Huffman, T. (1996)
"Archaeological Evidence for Climatic Change During the Last 2000 Years in Southern Africa." *Quaternary International* 33: 55-60.

Klapwijk, M. (1974)
A Preliminary Report on Pottery from the North-eastern Transvaal, South Africa. *South African Archaeological Bulletin* 29: 19-23.

Lamb, H. (1972)
Climate: Past, Present, and Future, Vol. 1. Fundamentals and Climate Now. London: Methuen

Livingstone, D. (1975)
"Late Quaternary Climatic Changes in Africa." *Annual Review of Economy and Systematics* 6: 249-280.

MacPhee, R. and Burney, D. (1991)
"Dating of Modified Femora of Extinct Dwarf Hippopotamus From Southern Madagascar: Implications for Constraining Human Colonisation and Vertebrate Extinction Events." *Journal of Archaeological Science* 18: 695-706.

Maley, J. (1993)
"The Climatic and Vegitational History of the Equatorial Regions of Africa During the Upper Quaternary." In Shaw, T., Sinclair, P. Andah, B. and Okpoko, A. (eds.), *The Archaeology of Africa*, 43-52. New York: Routledge.

Msemwa, P. (1994)
"An Ethnoarchaeological Study of Shellfish Collection in a Complex Urban Setting."
Unpublished *Ph.D* Dissertation., Brown University, Providence, R.I.

Odner, K. (1972)
"Excavations at Narosura, a Stone Bowl Site in the Southern Kenya Highlands." *Azania* 7:
25-92.

Pwiti, G. (1996)
Continuity and Change. Studies in African Archaeology 13. Uppsala: Societas Archaeologica
Upsaliensis.

Pwiti, G. (2002)
Further Observations on the Culture History and Spatial Behaviour of Prehistoric Farming
Communities of the Mid-Zambezi Valley, Northern Zimbabwe. In Chami, F. Pwiti, G. and
Radimilahy, C. (eds.), *Southern Africa and the Swahili World.*, 98-105. Studies in the African
Past 2. Dar-es-Salaam: Dar-es-Salaam University Press Ltd.

Robertshaw, P. and Taylor, D. (2000)
Climate Change and the rise of Political Complexity in Western Uganda. *Journal of African
History* 41:1-28.

Schmidt, P. (1997)
Iron Technology in East Africa. Bloomington: Indiana University.

Sinclair, P. (1987)
Space, Time and Social Formation. Uppsala: Societas Archaeologica Upsaliensis.

Sinclair, P. *et al.* (1993)
"A Perspective on Archaeological Research in Mozambique." In Shaw, T., Sinclair, P.,
Andah, B. and Okpoko, A. (eds.). *The Archaeology of Africa*, 410-431. New York: Routledge.

Sutton, J. (1977)
"The African Aqualithic." *Antiquity* 51(201): 25-34.

Tyson, P. and Lindesay, J. (1992)
"The Climate of the Last 2000 Years in Southern Africa." *The Holocene* 2: 271-278.

Whitelaw, G. and Moon, M. (1996)
The Ceramics and Distribution of Pioneer Agriculturists in KwaZulu-Natal. *Natal Museum
Journal of Humanities*, 8: 53-79.

2 Settlement Patterning in the Shashe-Limpopo Valley: Reflections From Surveys in Maramani and Lower Mzingwani Area

Munyaradzi Manyanga

INTRODUCTION

Archaeological research by the Archaeology Unit of the University of Zimbabwe in southern Zimbabwe has shifted its attention from the archaeologically rich Mateke Hills area to cover the valleys of the Shashe-Limpopo Rivers and its tributaries. This new research area, just to the north of Mapungubwe has yielded a wide range of sites, some of them extensive in size. Sites ranging from Stone Age to more recent historical periods show that the Shashe-Limpopo confluence and adjacent areas has accommodated human settlement for a long time. A number of the sites show close affinities with those that have been recorded on the South African and Botswana side of the Valley. This suggests that a related and an interacting community once occupied both sides of the Shashe-Limpopo rivers. While the area surveyed covered a distance of about 20km from the Shashe-Limpopo area, the general trend is that most Iron Age sites had a strong orientation towards the rivers over looking the flood plains. This strongly suggests a possibility of flood plain agriculture, a practice commonly used by local communities in the area today.

Research Background

The work presented here is a result of archaeological surveys that were conducted under the SIDA/SAREC-sponsored pilot phase of the Global

Archaeological Project. The work is in many ways an extension of the recently concluded Human Responses and Contribution to Environmental Change (HRAC) project in the Shashe-Limpopo basin. In its focus the pilot phase was built on the results and gains made under Urban Origins and HRAC Projects. Results from the HRAC project has shown that contrary to popular thought, Zimbabwe's southern lowveld has always attracted human settlements (Manyanga 2001). While the previous project focused on the area around the Mateke Hills and adjacent areas, the focus in the pilot phase of the Global project shifted further to the south and west to cover the Shashe and the Limpopo river valleys and their tributaries (Fig 2.1).

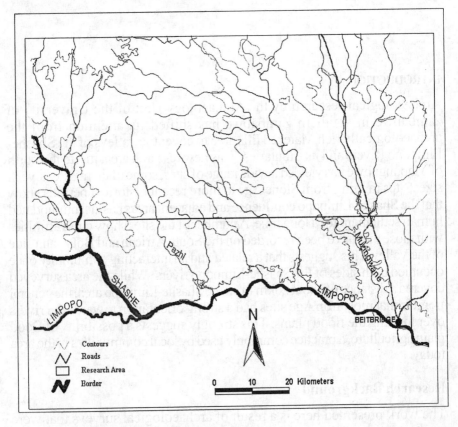

Fig 2.1: *The research area*

Preliminary work however covered an area stretching for over 120 km from Beitbridge Town to the Tuli circle and within a 15 km distance from the Limpopo/Shashe Rivers. The area generally coincides with some expeditions conducted by the Rhodesian Schools Exploration Society in the 1960s. Archaeological reports by the RSES's expeditions to Sentinel Ranch (1961) and Maramani (1967) provided a starting point in site location and characterisation in the research area. The area is adjacent to the popular sites of Schroda, K2 and Mapungubwe. While reference has been made to these sites in some detail, vague reference is made on sites on the Zimbabwean side of the Limpopo River. The surveys conducted were a way of bridging the void of information on archaeological sites on the Zimbabwean side of the Limpopo. These surveys also provided valuable complementary information to the University of Botswana archaeology team which is currently conducting archaeological research at the Shashe-Limpopo confluence, where the importance of alluvial corridors in settlement location has been highlighted (Tsheboeng 2001).

PHYSICAL SETTING

The dominant geological feature is the Karro system sandstone and the flood plains of the Limpopo River and its tributaries. Dolerite dykes can also be noted in the area. The physical landscape of the area is highly predictable with repeated sandstone ridges and open flat flood plains. The most outstanding feature of the area is the Homba hills which form a high ridge parallel to the Limpopo River. Further to the east towards the Mzingwani River, the area becomes more open bushveld with isolated sandstone kopjes.

The vegetation is dominated by the mopane woodland. Closer to the Limpopo and its tributaries is riverine vegetation. Important rivers in the research area include the Ipayi, Mushilachokwe and Mzingwani whose catchment area is the wetter Matopos. Annual rainfall is well below 400mm and most of the utilised moisture and water is brought from outside the valley through river flow. The area is also vulnerable to flooding. Hanisch (1980) points out that in a good rainy season the Shashe and the Limpopo rivers burst their banks resulting in flooding of their floodplain. The area has very high summer temperatures and is dry for most of the year. The current climatic conditions make the area highly unsuitable for rain fed agriculture. However the local populations today utilise the Limpopo valley flood plains as crop fields.

Archaeological Surveys

The archaeological surveys followed three main phases, namely: desktop assessment, reconnaissance survey and detailed survey. Information on the existing record of sites was compiled from the National Museum of Human Sciences in Harare. This yielded some sites that had been recorded mostly by the Rhodesian Schools Exploration Societies in the 1950s, 1960s and 1970s. Further information was sought from individuals in Maramani communal area and Nottingham, Sentinel and Border Ridge farms. This exercise yielded useful information and sites some of which did not appear in the official National Museums and Monuments site database. Through this process important site records by freelance archaeologists and private collections by farm owners were unearthed. This background study provided valuable information for designing the survey strategy in the research area. The main goals of the detailed surveys were to compile and build on the existing database of archaeological sites in the study area with the hope of understanding settlement types and patterning in the Shashe-Limpopo Valley. Surveys were conducted not only to identify sites but also to understand how societies in the valley used the landscape. Thus places with no traces of artefacts, features or ecofacts like open areas and disturbed vegetation zones were considered important landscape signatures.

The survey universe is defined by the country's southern Lowveld area, which is a broad zone below 600m above sea level. This covers quite a large area, implying the application of a sampling strategy. The southern extreme of the boundary is defined by the Shashe and Limpopo rivers. The surveys reflected in this report were conducted in the area between the Tuli Circle up to the Mzingwani/Limpopo confluence . The area targeted for surveys were those within a 15 km distance from the Shashe-Limpopo stretching from Beitbridge to the Tuli Circle. The following coverage was achieved during the surveys.

- 100% coverage within 0-5 km from the Shashe-Limpopo river;

- 40% coverage within 5-10 km from the Shashe-Limpopo river; and
- 20% coverage within 10-15 km from the Shashe-Limpopo river.

Where sampling had to be done, stratified random sampling was employed. This targeted areas including river valleys, sandstone or basalt hills and the open flat areas overlooking the river valleys. Surveys were based on 1: 50, 000 map sheets and the 1 km by 1 km boxes comprising the survey units. The surveyed area was conveniently divided into zones based on distances from the Shashe-Limpopo rivers. The area nearest to the rivers attracted 100% coverage and survey units were reduced as the distance from the rivers increased. Where a sample of less than 100% was carried out, the 1 km by 1 km boxes chosen took into consideration such attributes as the terrain, current land use and vegetation patterns. Data was captured on site recording forms which took note of such aspects as site location, GPS/ Grid Reference readings, altitude, cultural descriptions, features, vegetation, landforms, current land use and excavation potential.

The surveys were conducted by systematically walking over a targeted grid square and inspecting for archaeological sites. The procedure in the surveys began with field walking and site location using 1:50,000 survey maps and the GPS. This was followed by site documentation using site survey recording forms and photography. Depending with sites, *in situ* recording of interesting artefacts and features was also carried out. Since the exercise was also interested in establishing inter-site comparisons, surface collections, especially of pottery, was carried out. The data collected was the basis for dating and characterising the sites.

Site Types

Sites were classified on the basis of surface finds and features. Pottery and/ or architecture were the key determinants in site classification for Iron Age sites while stone tool types or art were useful in determining categories for Stone Age sites. The Iron Age sites were further classified into specific ceramic traditions established for the southern African sub region. The range of sites shows that the southern lowveld had a long history of human occupation probably beginning as early as the Early Stone Age up to the present. Whether this presents a case of continuity or the arrival of new population groups is an issue that may probably come to light after further detailed archaeological investigations.

The Stone Age

Very few Early Stone Age sites were recorded and these were characterised by isolated stone implements like cleavers, hand axes and flaked cobbles. Other sites had stone implements with Middle Stone Age characteristics, which portray flaking industries. These occurred on rocky areas especially those associated with dolerite. The Late Stone Age is well represented both in the form of stone implements and art. These sites were mostly noted on rock shelters. The rock art is in the form of engravings and paintings on sandstone. This period appears to have attracted earlier research especially at Mpato cave, which was excavated by Cooke and Simmons in 1969. Eastwood (1995) also conducted a preliminary survey and characterisation of the paintings in Nottingham and Sentinel Ranches. The majority of the art was executed by hunter-gatherer societies. Common depictions include animal figures, human figures and geometric designs. These include stylised male and female human figures and animals such as kudu, elephant, rhino, giraffe, warthog, buffalo, eland, sable, zebra, baboon, fish and birds. The art also has a number of symbols, the common one being the V-shaped and slash marks. An interesting observation is the engravings, which seem to portray footprints of medium and large sized bovids. Identifiable prints include those of hoofs of antelope, zebra and the human palm. Some of the cut marks appear to be consistent with the shape and form of common facial markings associated with the Venda. Not all the art in the area was executed by Late Stone Age hunter-gatherers but by Bantu speakers. Some of the paintings and engravings are associated with grain bins; an observation that made Eastwood *et al* (1995) to conclude that these might be associated with Iron Age Bantu communities.

Table 2.1: *Stone Age sites recorded*

Period/ Category	Early stone age	Middle stone age	Late stone age	Rock art
Number of sites	2	8	2	33

The Iron Age

These comprised the majority of sites recorded during the surveys. The sites were classified into 2 broad categories namely the Early Iron Age and the Later Iron Age (Table 2.7). However further sub divisions of these categories were done when diagnostic material was available to allow for further classification. Those Later Iron Age sites that were characterised by pottery scatter or sites abandoned in recent historical periods that were not diagnostic enough I here classified as other (Table 2.3).

Table 2.2: *Iron Age sites recorded*

Period/Category	Early Iron Age	Later Iron Age
Number Of Sites	6	171

Table 2.3: *Further classification of Iron Age sites*

Category	Zhizo	K2/mapungubwe (Central kraals)	Zimbabwe/Khami Phase (Walling & Enclosures)	19th Century Grain Bins	Venda-Historical	Other
Number of Sites	6	46	14	6	32	73

Early Iron Age

The Early Iron Age sites in areas that have been reported elsewhere are Malipati and Dombozanga (Phillipson 1977; Cooke 1958). Hanisch (1980) also reports that the lower levels at Mapungubwe yielded pottery that was classified as Early Iron Age. Very few Early Iron Age sites were recorded during the recent surveys in Maramani, Sentinel, Nottingham and Mzingwani areas. Huffman (*pers comm.*) related some sites noted during the recent surveys in Maramani to the terminal phase of the Early Iron Age characterised by the Zhizo Pottery. These were open sites with pottery that was characterised by both comb stamping and incision.

K2 and Mapungubwe

The majority of sites recorded are Later Iron Age sites especially those that relate to K2 and Mapungubwe. Differentiating K2 and Mapungubwe sites presented a major challenge during the surveys, especially if one bases the identification on ceramic types. Huffman (1974, 2000) believes that decoration placement, particularly the orientation of the arcades and triangles, is important in separating the periods. Because of this problem sites in this category, which could not be separated, were classified as K2/Mapungubwe.

K2 sites were mostly open mound sites, with a kraal taking a central position on the site (Fig 2.2). While some Mapungubwe sites were also open with the possibility of a central kraal, others were noted on hilltops with walling reflecting the establishment of a stratified society. However, not all sites with Mapungubwe pottery have evidence for social stratification. But a few, such as Dombo Tsvuka, reflect an elite residence in the form of stone walling which does not seem to play a defensive role. This site is located on a hill overlooking the Limpopo River. Access to the main site was limited, with only one easy but restricted passage on the north-western side of the hill. The rest of the sites were located on a ridge overlooking the Shashe flood plain and extending towards the Shashe-Limpopo confluence area. More sites were recorded on the sandstone ridges, which extend from the confluence area into Sentinel and Nottingham ranches. Most of the sites appear to be commoner's residence, cattle outposts or agricultural villages with central cattle byres. K2 and Mapungubwe sites have probably one of the most polished and finely executed ceramics.

The Zimbabwe Culture

The essence of this culture as noted by Huffman (2000: 14) is social stratification and associated ideology. The Zimbabwe cultural sequence in the Shashe-Limpopo is viewed as having begun with Mapungubwe (1220-1290), then Great Zimbabwe (1290-1450) and finally Khami (1450-1820. The later is thought to have broken up into other known historical groupings, of which the Shashe-Limpopo representations are the Venda. Research in the Soutpansberg and other areas south of the Limpopo has failed to locate any sites that can be attributed to the Great Zimbabwe phase. The area to the north of the Limpopo appears to reflect a different scenario. Earlier research in the Mateke hills and the adjacent Bubi and Limpopo valleys confirmed that a Zimbabwe culture is well represented in the Shashe-Limpopo valley (Manyanga 2000).

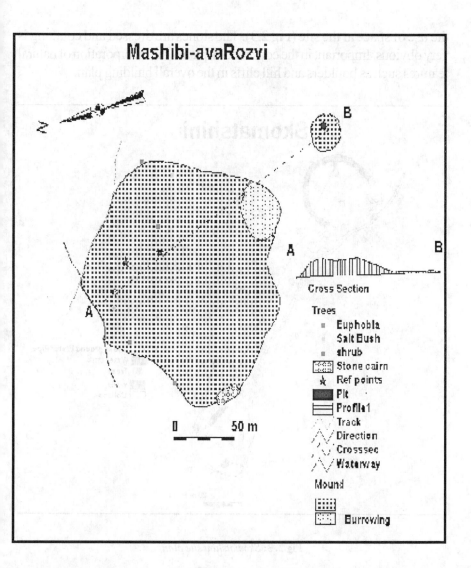

Fig 2.2: *Tobwani site*

A number of stone walled sites were noted in the area between the Shashe-Limpopo confluence and the Mzingwani-Limpopo confluence. Most of these Zimbabwe sites are located on hilltops with relatively flat tops. The walls are freestanding, circular with radiating walls, which appear to have demarcated the use of space at the site (Fig 2.3). The stones are dressed and coursing is very obvious. Important in the construction plan is the incorporation of natural features such as boulders and hill cliffs in the overall building plan.

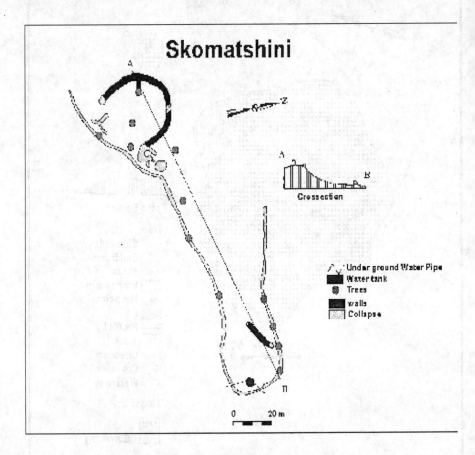

Fig 2. 3: *Skomatshini site plan*

There is no debate now about the occurrence of Khami phase sites in the Shashe-Limpopo valley. These have been noted in Botswana and in areas just south of the Limpopo. The Soutpansberg has the highest known cluster of these sites. A number of sites have been noted in Sentinel, Nottingham and in River Ranch. These comprise both commoner and elite sites with the characteristic panel and band ware. The *Village* 16 site best illustrates an elite Khami site in the research area. The elite residence has elaborate retaining walls on a small hill with a big kraal just below the hill. While much of the walling has collapsed, the walls appear to have formed ties. Of interest at the site is an engraved stone on the wall that has been a subject of many interpretations.

Venda

One of the most dominant ethnic groups of southern Zimbabwe and northern South Africa are the Venda. The current stronghold of the Venda is the Nzhelele valley and the Soutpansberg. While Venda traditions are complicated most however trace their origins with shona people north of the Limpopo. Venda society today is an amalgam of different groups, some of whom like the Ngona and Shona are thought to have been in the Shashe-Limpopo valley since the 13th and 14th Centuries (Loubser 1990:24-25). These traded and interacted with the Sotho-Tswana groups to the south of the Soutpansberg and traded with the coast leading to the development of the Venda language. A distinct Venda chiefdom is thought to have originated from Zimbabwe following the dispersion of the Tsingo ruling polity from central and southern Zimbabwe who established themselves south of the Limpopo in the Nzhelele valley around 1700 AD (von Sicard 1952; Loubser 1990). Some of the sites recorded in the survey area have been associated with the Venda and the modern inhabitants of the area relate a number of stone-walled sites along the Mzingwani River and Mushilashoko rivers to Venda history. Pottery from this site can be classified as Khami particularly the panel and band ware. The Chibombgwe Hill site shows that it was occupied over a long period of time and was probably an elite residence. A perimeter wall runs around the hill and on top of the main hill boulders and stone walling appear to have demarcated activity areas.

Grain Bins and Food Security

One of the most interesting archaeological finds of the research in the area is the grains storage facilities, generally referred to as grain bins. Recent surveys between the Shashe-Limpopo confluence and the Limpopo-Mzingwani confluence has revealed the existence of grain bins in caves situated at the bottom of a tree line on the sandstone ridges. The sites are mostly confined to the Homba hills on the Nottingham-Sentinel farms border. Six (6) sites were recorded in this area one of which had a cluster of twenty-six grain bins in a single cave. In total, forty-nine grain bins were noted from the 6 sites. The grain bins varied in size with the largest measuring 1.5m in diameter and 1.8 m in height. The smallest measured 0.3m in diameter and 0.4m in height. The bins were built using mopane wood poles and reeds, which were tied together using tree cambium rope. A wet *dhaka* plaster was then added to the frame. Some sites have been victims of fires whose source cannot be ascertained. The caves are fenced off using mopane poles. This fence has a well-defined entrance. Sorghum and millet have been noted in some of the grain bins.

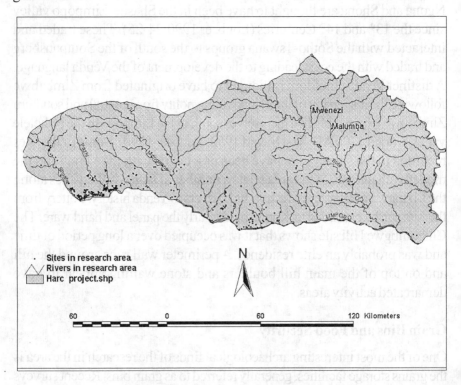

Fig 2.4: *Sited distribution in the research area*

The finding of these grain storage facilities has revived interest in the subject of pre/colonial food security as well as the socio/political conditions, which might have resulted in their construction. While 19th century conflicts pose as strong candidates for the circumstances leading to their construction, one has also to examine the vulnerability of the regions between the Zambezi and the Limpopo to both drought and occasional flooding, which impact negatively on agricultural practice.

Since the early 20th century, colonial administrators, ethnographers and archaeologists reported the existence of grain storage facilities mostly in cave or rock shelter locations on the Zimbabwe Plateau. Given the widespread accounts related to the Nguni, particularly Ndebele and Ngoni raids in the 19th century, these storage facilities are inextricably connected with them. They are thus considered part of a refuge culture, which is thought to have resulted in widespread movement across the plateau, with settlements being located on hilltops and mountains. There is a strong possibility that the grains bins played such an important role in as far as food security was concerned in the valley. Here food security related to both physical protection and the use of sound conservation methods of storage. The greatest threat to grain is moisture and pests. While discussions on grain bins have focussed on the need for concealed places against the cereal raiders, the aspect of moisture and pest-free conditions, which the concealed caves present, has often been overlooked. Probably this 19th century phenomenon derives so much from the earlier inhabitants of the area who grew cereals in the flood plains or traded it and stored in moisture free caves.

DISCUSSION

Settlement Patterning

To date reasonable survey samples have been conducted in the Shashe-Limpopo Basin. A total of 219 new sites were added to the site database of the research area. While the area surveyed covered a distance of about 15km from the Shashe-Limpopo area, the general trend is that most of the sites had a strong orientation towards the rivers, alluvial corridors and the flood plains of the Shashe and Limpopo rivers. Despite the climatic deterrents today, it looks as if the valleys have always attracted or accommodated human settlement for a long time. A considerable portion of the valley area between the Shashe-Limpopo and Mzingwani-Limpopo confluences are important receiving areas in terms of moisture and soil nutrients. Observation emanating from the effect of cyclone *Eline* and past river regimes shows that the Shashe-Limpopo valley is an area which is to a large extent influenced by developments outside the valley itself. This could have been important in the past especially when the environment in the valley itself would have significantly deteriorated. The Shashe-Limpopo valley, with a favourable catchment area, would then have saved as an important focal point for human groups. The outside influences could also have brought adverse effects, which could have meant important consideration in settlement location.

K2 and Mapungubwe sites are oriented towards the rivers and the floodplains. The sites are mostly on natural mounds, which resemble natural terraces. It appears as if settlements were located on those areas with the least chances of flooding while at the same time being near the flooded areas. Where located, these formed a dense cluster and household units formed a circular pattern around a kraal, which on the surface approximate Kuper's (1980) southern Bantu cattle pattern. The most outstanding feature on these sites was the extensive kraals used to single out household units. This method of defining household units however has limitations in that it is common among traditional livestock keepers to change and rotate the location of kraals in a single season in response to dung accumulations and moisture in the kraal.

It is common knowledge that settlement location is not random but is determined by a number of considerations that relate to subsistence among others. The idea that the floodplains could have been utilised as crop field comes into mind, but such supposition needs to be tested further in the field. Available data from the valley shows that millet and sorghum were some of the important crops in the valley (Johnnson 1998). However the current rainfall regime of less than 400mm per annum cannot sustain the growing of these crops without irrigation. Climatic change models have been suggested as well as the importance of circumscribed environments (Manyanga 2000). The two explanations still do not provide adequate explanations for the area under discussion. The climatic model accounts possibly for the period 900AD-1300AD associated with the Medieval Warm Epoch, a period associated with increasing rainfall and economic prosperity. How then can one explain subsistence in the Shashe-Limpopo valley before and after this period, when climatic conditions were poor and the valley still attracted human settlement? The environmental circumscription model (Manyanga *et. al.* 2000) lacks relevance, as there are no such environmental zones in the area under discussion. This leaves the possibility of floodplain agriculture as a strong possibility in the Shashe-Limpopo valley. We know that floods take place in the area and that the local population make use of the benefits of floods in both subsistence and commercial agricultural enterprises. Communal people in Maramani, for example, use the flood plains as crop fields, winter grazing areas, hunting and gathering and extracting palm sap which makes a potent wine. Interestingly enough, the people utilise the ridges, long used by their ancestors, as settlement locations. They are very much aware of the dangers of building settlements in the floodplains.

Most of the K2 and Mapungubwe sites were recorded in open areas characterised by the saltbush. The saltbush formed an interface with Mopane woodland. The later vegetation zone however did not yield any meaningful archaeological sites. This pattern made site location highly predictable. The extent of human activity was in most cases defined by the extent of the saltbush, which is known to be secondary vegetation. Mopane is highly sensitive to human exploitation hence its colony begins were human impact was at its minimum. Another possibility is that the mopane defines the limits of those areas that could be utilised for floodplain agriculture.

Zimbabwe culture sites are all located on flat hilltops close to main water sources. These command a wonderful view of the surroundings. These sites are still located in the same broad areas as the K2 and Mapungubwe sites although settlements shifted from the terraces to the more elevated hilltops. Whether this is a reflection of a major ideological shift is something that cannot be established at this stage of research. The sites are elite residence as they demonstrate a major investment in terms of effort and resource. Some of the walling is quite extensive and does reflect the input of a broader society in their construction. These are obviously elite residence and more question again arise from these. Would decisions that relate to settlement location and meant to reduce the dangers of natural catastrophe like flooding, be considered a monopoly of a few individuals in society? These are issues that arise out of the current surveys data, which will possibly come to light with further investigations.

The sites represent a considerable period of occupation beginning with the Stone Age until more recent periods. It is probably premature to discuss issues that relate to settlement transformation at this stage. However, information gathered from the Mateke hills during the earlier phases of this search and survey results under this discussion seem to suggest continuous occupation in the valley. We have representations of sites that relates to the so called leopard's Kopje Tradition with its various phases, Zimbabwe Culture Tradition and sites reflecting the more recent historical periods. It is likely that the declining environmental conditions in the valley would have discouraged settlement in the valley, but it is not everybody who would have moved. Those who stayed would have made use of opportunities brought by flooding and other resources with an orientation towards the river systems. What seems likely is that the progressive ceramic groupings and site types noted from about 700 AD to 1800AD represents continuity and the appearance of other ceramic styles and types only reflects the level of social interactions among the society.

CONCLUSION

It is apparent that the survey data has brought more questions than answers in as far as the debates on the Shashe-Limpopo valley is concerned. What the survey data has managed to allude to, are the range of sites and how these are located in relationship to other environmental considerations. The most important consideration in settlement location appears to have been access to water sources water sources. It has also been shown that there was a strong correlation between the sites and the floodplains which has brought to the fore the idea of possible floodplain agriculture. The challenge is to adopt research strategies and approaches that can interrogate the Shashe-Limpopo landscape with a view of understanding the settlement transformation and subsistence in the valley. Crucial in the research endeavours is an approach, which looks at the Shashe-Limpopo Rivers not as a barrier to human interaction but as a place for resilience, creativity, convergence and cultural exchange. Previous research focus appears to have been dictated by modern political boundaries and the political divide and isolation until the early 1990s. This was an artificial separation whose premise was based on

BIBLIOGRAPHY

Cooke, C. K. (1958)
"A Preliminary Survey of the Archaeology of the Mateke Hills Area." Unpublished report of Rhodesian Schools Exploration Society-Matabeleland 1958, 55-83.

Cooke, C. K. (1966a)
"Archaeology Report." Unpublished report of the Rhodesian Schools Exploration Society-Shashi Expedition 1966, 18-19.

Fouche, L. (ed.) (1937)
Mapungubwe:Ancient Bantu Civilisations on the Limpopo. Cambridge. Cambridge University Press.

Gardner, G.A. (1963)
Mapungubwe. Volume II. Van Schalk: University of Pretoria.

Garlake, P. (1966)
"Iron Age Archaeology." Unpublished report of the Rhodesian Schools Exploration Society-Shashi Expedition 1966: 19-22.

Garlake, P. (1968)
"Test Excavations at Mapela Hill, Near the Shashi River, Rhodesia." *Arnoldia* 3, 1(29.

Hanisch, E. (1980)
"An Archaeological Interpretation of Certain Iron Age Sites in the Shashi/Limpopo Valley." Unpublished MA thesis, University of Pretoria.

Huffman, T. N. (1993)
"Broederstroom and the Central Cattle Pattern." *South African Journal of Science.* 89: 220-7.

Huffman, T.N. (1974)
"The Leopard's Kopje Tradition." *Museum Memoir* No 6. Rhodesia: National Museums and Monuments of Zimbabwe.

Huffman, T.N. (2000)
"Mapungubwe and the Origins of the Zimbabwe Culture." *The Southern African Archaeological Society Godwin Series,* 8: 14-29

Jonsson, J. (1998)
"Early Plant Economy in Zimbabwe." Fil. Lic thesis. Uppsala: Department of Archaeology and Ancient History.

Kupper, A. (1980)
"Symbolic Dimensions of the Southern Bantu Homestead." *Africa,* 50 (1): 8-23.

Lane, P., & Segobye A. (eds) (1998)
Ditswa Mmung: The Archaeology of Botswana. Gaborone: Pula Press.

Loubser, J. (1990)
"Oral Traditions, Archaeology and the History of Venda Mitupo." *African Studies,* 49 (2): 13-42

Maggs, T. (2000)
South African Archaeological Society. Goodwin Series 8

Manyanga, M. (2000)
Choices and Constraints. Animal Resource Exploitation in South Eastern Zimbabwe

Manyanga, M, I. Pikirayi & W. Ndoro. (2000)
"Coping With Dryland Environments. Preliminary Results From Mapungubwe and Zimbabwe Phase Sites in the Mateke Hills, South Eastern Zimbabwe." *The Southern African Archaeological Society Godwin Series*, 8: 69-77

Pwiti, G. (1997a)
"The Origins and Development of Stone Building Cultures of Zimbabwe." In Dewey, W. J. (ed.), *Legacies of Stone: Past and Present*, Vol. 1: 77-95. Brussels: Royal Museum for Central Africa.

Robinson, K. R. (1961)
"The Archaeology of the Sentinel Expedition, 1961." Unpublished report of the Rhodesian Schools Exploration Society-Sentinel Expedition 1961, 14-18.

Summers, R. (1960)
Environment and Culture in Southern Rhodesia. Cambridge: Cambridge University Press.

Tsheboeng, A. (2001)
Late Iron Age Human Responses and Contribution to Environmental Change in the Shashi-Limpopo River Basin: North Eastern Botswana. In Chami, F., Pwiti, G and C, Radimilahy (eds), *People, Contacts and the Environment in the African Past*. Dar es Salaam: Dar es Salaam University Press Ltd.

Tyson, P. D. & R. Lindsey (1992)
The Climate of the Last 2000 Years in Southern Africa. *Holocene* (2): 271- 278.

Voigt, E. A. (1983)
Mapungubwe: An Archaeozoological Interpretation of an Iron Age Community. Pretoria: Transvaal Museum.

Von Sicard, H. (1952)
Ngoma Lungundu: Eine Africanische bundeslade. Uppsala Studia Ethnopraphica Upsalensi.

3 Forests, Farmers and Furnaces: The Potential Ecological Impact of Prehistoric Mining and Metallurgy in Zimbabwe

Lorraine Swan

INTRODUCTION

Ecological problems in parts of Africa are largely considered as caused by recent land use practices. However, some problems of ecological imbalance began as a result of human activities centuries ago (e.g. Lane *et al* 2001). As the social sciences begin to depart from a conventional view of ecology where traditional societies existed in a balanced ecology, disrupted by modern change, it has been suggested that an interdisciplinary approach which acknowledges interaction between culture and environment should be adopted (Scoones 1999). Archaeological research in particular is a branch of social science which by nature explores change through time. Dynamic relationships between past societies and their ecological setting have been the subject of archaeological studies which have incorporated information from various scientific approaches to explain shifting archaeological settlement patterns.

Considerations of environmental change as an important factor both resulting from and influencing social change in southern Africa has proved a useful tool in archaeological interpretation of the past. The relationship between climate change at the beginning of the Little Ice Age, the abandonment of Mapungubwe and succession of Great Zimbabwe as the regional capital (Huffman 1996; 2000) is the most obvious example. Environmental degradation caused by over-exploitation of the environment by a large population concentrated at Great Zimbabwe has been offered as one of the principal explanations for the decline of the Great Zimbabwe state (Garlake 1970; Huffman 1977) with the impact of deforestation around the site still evident now (Huffman 1977; Pikirayi 2001). A similar explanation has been suggested in the case of the move of Mutapa centres from the Zimbabwean plateau northwards into the Zambezi Valley in the early eighteenth century (Pikirayi 2001).

Other responses to environmental change besides population movement have been put forward. Recent archaeological research which aimed at examining human responses and contributions to environmental change in southern Africa identified changes in subsistence practices and resource use, contemporary with climatic changes (Pwiti 2001). Extrapolating from the climate-based explanation for the demise of Mapungubwe and rise of Great Zimbabwe at the end of the thirteenth century, Manyanga (2000) suggested that subsistence strategies in the Mateke Hills altered in response to climate change. Hence the response to environmental change in this case may have been increased reliance upon wild rather than domestic food resources. In other cases, not only in Zimbabwe but also in other parts of southern Africa, manufacturing industries based on local mineral resources were developed to supplement agricultural subsistence and as an insurance in the event of agricultural failure, particularly where the environment was marginal for agricultural production (Prendergast 1979a; Maggs 1982; Swan 1994).

Some of the most important contributions to explain socio-economic systems which operated in the historic Zimbabwe culture emphasise Zimbabwe's inherently unpredictable climate patterns. Society responded to this difficulty by accruing wealth in livestock and by optimising the potential production of different parts of the country such as areas where there were deposits of iron, gold, copper or salt, or hunting particularly to obtain ivory, in order to participate in trade (Beach 1977). Redistribution of produce may have been socially mediated by the central authority (Vogel 1990). Management of land and resources may have been the foundation for the emergence of social complexity in the region and could have enabled elites to sustain central political authority (Pikirayi 2001). Another response was ideological, reinforcing the importance of religious practices such as rainmaking ceremonies and of the spiritual role of leadership.

In view of the region's fragile ecosystem, environmental causes for population dispersal and decline of complex societies are logical. Whilst overgrazing and cutting of forests for field clearance, firewood and tobacco curing are usually considered the principal factors causing environmental imbalance, the impact of traditional African metallurgy must have been significant (Friede 1983) and should be considered. This chapter focuses on the impact which the mining and metallurgical industry may have had on the environment and examines the extent to which it is possible to draw conclusions about the ecological impact of this aspect of past human activities. After examining previous literature on the topic, this paper investigates the potential for applying some of the research methods used elsewhere to the Zimbabwean situation.

THE ECOLOGICAL IMPACT OF METALLURGY IN AFRICA

It appears that whilst some areas achieved a sustainable balance between charcoal requirements for smelting and tree regeneration (Friede 1983), other areas did not. The need to seriously consider the profound effect of environmental change on traditional industry has been emphasised, particularly as an important factor explaining the demise of West African iron and copper industries in the nineteenth century (Goucher 1981; Herbert 1984). Climate change and deforestation, European trade in specific hardwood species and continued pressure to supply charcoal for smelting, which affected the rate of forest regeneration, (Goucher 1981; Herbert 1984; de Barros 1986) are some of the factors which eventually led to increased reliance upon European metal products imported into West Africa. In parts of Africa the availability of European scrap iron meant an end to traditional smelting but continuation of smithing practices (Prendergast 1972; Mackenzie 1975; Schmidt 1997b). Other explanations for the discontinuance of a traditional metallurgical industry were centuries of forest clearance for agriculture, centralisation of iron production centres or abandonment of iron production areas caused by movement of populations into mountainous areas to evade raiding by neighbouring groups (de Barros 1986). Nonetheless the fact that French colonial authorities introduced legal measures to control deforestation in both Togo and Senegal, particularly forbidding iron-smelting in Togo, indicates that the significant ecological impact of the iron-smelting industry was recognised (Goucher 1981; de Barros 1986).

The quantity of charcoal required for smelting, which could vary between 80 kilograms and 1455 kilograms per smelt dependent upon the type of ore smelted and the technology used (Miller 1997), probably consumed a greater proportion of forest resources than any other aspect of mining or metallurgy. Timber would have been required in mining operations for fire setting, props, ladders, tools such as wedges, scoops, digging sticks and gad handles and containers such as buckets, as well as for roasting gold ore prior to mechanical concentration and separation (Summers 1969; Swan 2002). Samples of wood found in archaeological mining deposits at Copper Queen Mine were tentatively identified as species which still existed on and around the mine in recent times, suggesting that the early mining activities had had little impact on the type of climax vegetation present (Swan 2002). It is unlikely that any aspect of mining and metallurgy would have such a profound impact on forest areas as the production of charcoal for smelting and smithing iron and copper ores, and for domestic use. In a modern analogy, 18000 tons of charcoal were produced annually on the Zambian copper belt, of which 5000 tons were used in the copper refineries and the rest for domestic consumption (Mihalyi 1972).

Very large slag mounds found in parts of Mali, Togo, Cameroon and at Meroe were evidence for intensive, centralised iron production (Haaland 1980; Goucher 1981; de Barros 1986). Deriving relationships between variables from ethnographic models, the dimensions of slag heaps have been used to estimate the quantity of ore which would have been smelted and the quantity of charcoal consumed in the smelting process. This in turn produced tentative quantitative information about the use of forest resources with the conclusion that the enormous quantities of wood required to provide charcoal to support an iron smelting and smithing industry inevitably exhausts the local supply of wood (Haaland 1980; Goucher 1981). It would be useful to develop these models so that fuel quantities could be estimated on the basis of slag remains found at archaeological sites. Table 3.1 attempts to compare the variables recorded by several researchers. My own calculations are shown in italics. In practice it is difficult to compare the examples given. The variables would be altered dependent upon the following factors:

a) Type of ore, for example smelting processes observed in Malawi were

Table 3.1: *Quantities of slag, iron, ore, charcoal and wood recorded by different researchers*

Example	Reference	Wood	Charcoal	Wood: Charcoal ratio	Ore	Charcoal:ore ratio	Bloom	Iron	Charcoal: iron ratio	Slag	Charcoal :slag ratio
Dapaa site	Goucher (1981)	(8384 tonnes) 307431 trees (60 pounds (27 kg) dry weight per tree)	(838,4 tonnes?)	Assumed 10:1						210 tonnes or 2000 m³	Assumed 4:1 (by weight?)
	Friede (1983)	2 to 3 medium-sized acacias	80 to 90 kg					1,5 kg hoe			
Darfur smelters	Haaland (1985)		4 volume units (1380 kg per 4 m³)		2 volume units	(2:1) by volume		1 volume unit		1 volume unit (106,82 kg per 1 m³)	4:1 by volume (13:1 by weight)
Mema	Haaland (1985)	480000 m³		Assumed 4:1 by volume						30000 m³ (3205 tonnes)	
Meroe	Haaland (1985)	449600 m³								25600 m³ (2735 tonnes)	
Phoka, Malawi 1982	van der Merwe & Avery (1987)	88 m³	1 tonne					4 hoes + some smaller tools			
Chulu, Malawi	van der Merwe & Avery (1987)		1450 kg		75 kg	19,3:1	91 kg sponge		15,9:1 to bloom		
Phoka 1985	van der Merwe & Avery (1987)		1000 kg		55 kg	18,18:1	75 kg sponge		13,3:1 to bloom		
Kasungu bloomery 1982 *	Gordon & Killick (1993)		3200 pounds (1453 kg)		165 pounds (75 kg)	19,4:1 by weight		Assumed 30 kg	Assumed 48:1 by weight?		

* Figures based on van der Merwe and Avery (1987)

designed for low-grade ore with a secondary smelt and was demanding of fuel and labour (van der Merwe and Avery 1987). Although the charcoal-ore ratio observed there was 18:1 or 19:1 it was noted that a common ratio was 5:1 (Gordon and Killick 1993).

b) Type of smelting technology, for example the natural-draft method is noted as less fuel-efficient than the forced-draft method because furnaces drew in air much more slowly than forced-draft types so the time taken to produce an iron bloom was longer and heat loss was proportionally greater (Gordon and Killick 1993).

c) Efficiency of the charcoal-burning method. The commercial forestry industry in Zimbabwe currently achieves reduction rates of 4,7 tonnes of wood at dry weight (about 25% moisture content) to 1 tonne of charcoal, and estimates that traditional methods would achieve rates of roughly 7:1. Traditional methods in use on the Zambian copper belt (Mihalyi 1972) produced about 1 tonne of charcoal from about 12 to 20 tonnes of wood (assuming that 1 m^3 of dry wood weighs about 600 kg and that the Zambian charcoal outputs are measured in imperial tons and not metric tonnes, in which case the wood-charcoal ratio would be higher). The reduction ratio of 88 m^3 of wood to one tonne of charcoal recorded in Malawi (van der Merwe and Avery 1987) is extremely high. Discarding much of the fine charcoal (Schmidt 1997b) would obviously increase the ratio. Goucher (1981) assumed a ratio of 10:1, presumably by weight, and Haaland's (1985) assumption of 4:1 by volume is about 7:1 by weight.

d) Density of the wood. One of the most important variables is the species of trees which were selected for charcoal (Table 3.2). Observers of traditional African iron-smelting practices in the early twentieth century noted the care taken in the selection of woods for charcoal (Wainwright 1945). Some authors simply referred to hard woods or to species with sufficient heat-generating attributes (Weeks 1913; Haaland 1985; Lane et al 2001). The properties of some species were conducive to a successful and efficient smelt by virtue of their chemical properties which could act as a flux (Schmidt 1997b) or the heat generated and these tended to have longer growing periods, hence increasing the rate of regeneration (Goucher

1981). One analysis of smelting charcoal identified a "soup" of different species apparently as a result of off-cuts collected from the margins of areas cleared for settlements and fields (Schmidt 1997a).

e) Degree of drying out of the wood before burning. For instance in Buhaya, the wood was burned wet (Schmidt 1997b). Goldsmith and Carter (1981) give densities for a list of indigenous species at 12% moisture content.

Table 3.2: *Species of trees that were selected for iron smelting or forging*

Species	Reference	Region used	Source of evidence	Density per m³ at 12% moisture content (Goldsmith & Carter 1981)
Pentaclethra macrophylla; Erythrophloeum guineense; Cylicodiscus gabunensis; Eurypetalum tessmannii; Irvingia grandifolia	Tessman (1913)	West Africa	Observation	
Olea chrysophylla (for smelting); *Juniperus procera* (for forging)	Hobley (1922)	Kenya	Observation	
Acacia sp.	Wainwright (1945)	West Africa	Ethnographic research	
mbonda *Combretum apiculatum;* muraradwayi; munyunya *Monotes engleri;* mukarati *Burkea africana*	Prendergast *(1972)*	Shurugwi, Zimbabwe	Ethnographic research	935 kg
myange (muwanga?) *Pericopsis angolensis?;* mushava	Mackenzie (1975)	Hwedza, Zimbabwe	Ethnographic research	908 kg

Species	Reference	Region used	Source of evidence	Density per m³ at 12% moisture content (Goldsmith & Carter 1981)
Monotes engleri; mukarate Burkea africana				935 kg
Burkea africana; Acacia sp.; Prosopis africana; Zizyphus mucronata	Goucher (1981)	West Africa	Ethnographic research	935 kg
Olea africana (wild olive); Spirostachys africana (tamboti)	Maggs (1982)	Natal, S. Africa	Oral tradition	1160 kg 908 kg
Acacia caffra, Acacia ataxacantha or Acacia burkei	Maggs (1982)	Natal, S. Africa	Preliminary results of charcoal analysis	
Syzygium guineense	Schmidt (1997b)	Buhaya, Kagera region, north west Tanzania	Ethnographic research	

Substituting a measured slag density of 107 kg per 1 m³ (Goucher 1981) and a measured charcoal density of 345 kg per 1 m³ for particle sizes ranging from dust to pieces of 2 cm diameter, then the examples in Table 1 show that a single smelt using between 80 kg and 1500 kg of charcoal may consume very roughly 600 kg to 30 tonnes or 1 m³ to 50 m³ of wood and may produce 6 kg to 120 kg of slag.

Having established the quantity of wood required for smelting, the hectarage of land affected by deforestation could be quantified if the biomass per unit of area of the species selected, the growth rate of these species and the rate of forest regeneration were known. On the Zambian copper belt one hectare of forest comprising mainly Brachystegia and Iserbolinia species gave roughly 10 to 15 tonnes of charcoal (Mihalyi 1972). Forest regeneration rates appear to vary widely. Schmidt's (1997b) work in Buhaya suggests such devastating ecological damage that forests had only partially recovered after a period of about 600 years. If the preferred species were thinly dispersed through a forest, the overall impact on the environment would be less dramatic than if there were a majority of suitable species in a forest, obviously leading to total deforestation of a more concentrated area and correspondingly severe erosion (Haaland 1985). In fact opening up the forest canopy by selectively felling larger trees allows sunlight to reach forest undergrowth and encourages growth of seedlings, enhancing regeneration (Chigwerewe 1996).

It must also be remembered that slag from a smelting furnace is the product of only one stage of the metallurgical process. More slag was removed from the bloom during the forging stage. Some smelting technologies incorporated slag from previous smelts (van der Merwe & Avery 1987). Hence the quantity of slag seen at a smelting site would be a minimum product of a smelting procedure.

Metal producers must have found solutions to the continued need for charcoal supply in the face of depleted forests. Communities responded by moving location periodically (Haaland 1985), abandoning deforested areas then reoccupying them later with revised smelting techniques (Schmidt 1997a), or specialisng so that smelters were located close to ore sources, smiths to sources of stone for tools and charcoal burners close to remnant forests (de Barros 1986). Technical innovations included preheating the air supply by extending tuyeres further into the furnace to increase fuel efficiency (Goucher 1981) or using swamp grass in place of charcoal in the furnace bottom (Schmidt 1997a). Some communities eventually resorted to metal goods imported from neighbouring areas or from Europe (Goucher 1981; de Barros 1986; Schmidt 1997b).

THE POTENTIAL FOR FURTHER RESEARCH IN ZIMBABWE

Theoretically it should be possible to apply in Zimbabwe the models used in other parts of Africa to study the potential impact of metallurgy on the environment. Initially a regional chronology for iron-smelting in Zimbabwe must be established. Prendergast's (1974) review of the available evidence remains useful in this regard although more recent research has increased the available data. The handful of smelting sites which have been excavated and dated appear to show a gradual change in furnace type and smelting technology through time. Furnace types used by the earliest iron-producers in eastern and southern Africa are said to have been deep, cylindrical pit shapes used for primary smelting and shallow, dish-shaped furnaces used for secondary smelting (Collett 1985). Furnace remains from this period have not yet been recovered in Zimbabwe, where the earliest furnace remains were found at Darwendale, Buhwa, Mazowe and Arcturus and dating from the early eleventh to the mid fifteenth centuries AD (Prendergast 1983, 1975, 1979a; van der Merwe 1978; Swan 1997). These represent furnace structures which had relatively large diameters and multiple tuyere holes. They may relate to natural-draft, shaft furnaces which are a common African type (Cline 1937; Gordon & Killick 1993) but were not recognised in Zimbabwe until the Hunyani Survey (Prendergast 1975). A date of BP 1010 ± 40 (GrA-9244), which calibrates to the early eleventh to mid twelfth centuries AD, for the furnace excavated at Arcturus (Swan 1997) can now be added to the list of large-diameter furnaces which probably used natural draft. The charcoal sample from which the date derives was collected from the original ground surface at the bottom of accumulated smelting debris outside the furnace base. Ndoro (1994) noted evidence for large-scale iron-working in large, natural-draft furnaces to the south-west of Great Zimbabwe and it would be useful to compare the date of these with those of bellows-driven furnaces with small quantities of slag and tuyeres found in the same area.

Ethnographic examples (Prendergast 1972; Mackenzie 1975) and excavated, dated furnaces (Prendergast 1977; 1978; 1979a; 1979b) show clearly that iron-smelting in Zimbabwe from the early eighteenth to the early twentieth centuries used forced-draft furnaces. It has been suggested that a pit type with a domical cap and usually associated with drum bellows was replaced around the seventeenth century by beehive types which used goat-skin bag bellows (Mackenzie 1974). An example of the pit and domical cap type furnace was excavated in north-western Zimbabwe where associated pottery indicated a mid-second millennium date (Garlake 1971) and another in south-western Zimbabwe, associated with Leopard's Kopje pottery, may have been as early as the tenth to fourteenth centuries AD (Robinson 1953). An open bowl type of furnace was probably in use in some areas during the early colonial period (Prendergast 1972).

The large, earlier, natural-draft furnaces imply a scale of production beyond the immediate needs of the group (Prendergast 1972). It has recently been suggested that agricultural output increased at the end of the first millennium and beginning of the second millennium AD with the development of social and political complexity, which stimulated economic and technological responses including increase in iron production to meet the demand for exchange goods, for tools to build zimbabwe structures and for gold mining and to provide the requisite agricultural tools as settlement distribution expanded onto heavy, red, fertile soils (Pikirayi 2001). By continuing to examine furnace typology, chronology and distribution, further research could investigate whether the larger capacity iron-smelting furnaces of this period were a response to the increased demand for iron, or whether iron production became more centralised around the higher-grade ore resources. Alternatively the use of this furnace type may have been dictated by cultural rather than functional requirements. Since natural-draft furnaces were less fuel-efficient than forced-draft furnaces, the possibility that the combination of increased production and increased fuel-to-ore ratio may have introduced pressure on woodland resources at this period could be considered.

As mentioned above, environmental impact has been offered as one of the explanations for the decline of Great Zimbabwe in the fifteenth century. Further research might consider whether adaptation to more fuel-efficient forced-draft furnace types was one response to the need for resource conservation. A more likely explanation for this change in the mid second millennium is a reduction in the scale of smelting, limiting production to the needs of the immediate community, caused by economic decline and population dispersal. Nonetheless, the hypothesis of ecological damage could be tested through analysis of pollen and charcoal. Charcoal from smelting sites could be studied to detect changes in species selection through time, using the methodology applied in Buhaya (Schmidt 1997a), and bearing in mind the shortcomings of charcoal analysis in this type of application (Shackleton & Prins 1993). A prerequisite to this type of analysis would be the compilation of suitable comparative material from the region. Pollen analytical studies from iron-producing areas should give information not only about changes in species present but also about forest regeneration rates (Haaland 1985). An interdisciplinary approach incorporating palynology and archaeology has been encouraged (Taylor & Marchant 1995). Besides pollen cores collected from permanently waterlogged situations such as peaty deposits in the eastern highlands of Zimbabwe (Tomlinson 1973) and swamp sediments in Uganda (Taylor & Marchant 1995), pollen analysis has been successfully applied using samples from coprolites in deposits associated with pans in South Africa (Scott & Brink 1992), from hyrax middens in Namibia (Scott 1996) and from dry cave deposits (Carrion 1992a; 1992b; Carrion et al 1995).

Charcoal burning for metal production is unlikely to have contributed much to the environmental deterioration around Great Zimbabwe itself. Detailed research is required to investigate suggestions of large-scale iron-smelting at the site (Herbert 1996). At present Great Zimbabwe appears to contrast with early first millennium Buhaya where social stratification may have been a result of control over iron production by certain groups (Schmidt 1997a) and the Kingdom of Ghana where control over centralised iron production and hence over production of superior weaponry facilitated the establishment and maintenance of a central political authority (Haaland 1980). In Zimbabwe iron-working was a widespread activity (Prendergast 1974) and the central authority was more likely developed and maintained by control of widely distributed resources. Relatively large-scale metal production industries developed around some ore resources or on the basis of metallurgical expertise such as that recorded among the Njanja in the early 20th century (Mackenzie 1975) and it is in these areas that evidence for the potential impact of the metallurgical industry on forest resources could be sought.

Among the Njanja, a full day of smelting produced sufficient iron to produce 12 to 20 hoes, and hoes varied from 1 kg to more than 2 kg each (Mackenzie 1975). Assuming that smelting took place on a minimum of 50 days from May to September each year, then the Njanja may have produced a minimum of 700 to 1000 hoes each season. Since a 1,5 kg hoe required 80 to 90 kg of charcoal or 2 to 3 medium-sized *Acacias* (Friede 1983), annual charcoal consumption may have been a minimum of 1400 to 2000 medium sized trees. Smelting furnaces were concentrated in one area of water and charcoal supply to facilitate ore delivery and continued in use from one year to another, being sheltered during rains and repaired as necessary. We are not told whether exhaustion of fuel supply prompted occasional movement of the smelting factory. The industry declined as a result of colonial administrative restrictions. Njanja territory subsequently became communal land so continued use for subsistence agriculture would mask earlier deforestation caused by smelting consumption.

Societies in Zimbabwe, including the Njanja, were primarily farmers who developed additional, part-time metal-producing industries (Beach 1977). When ores were smelted close to the place where they were mined and away from settlements other than perhaps temporary mining camps then deforestation in the area could be a result of the combined mining and smelting activities. In instances where ores were transported and smelted close to settlements such as nineteenth century Katanga (Herbert 1984), mid-first millennium Kansanshi (Bisson 1974) and nineteenth century Dikulwe (National Archives files), deforestation as a result of field clearance and domestic requirements would be indistinguishable from the impact of metallurgical requirements and would need to be considered in combination.

20th century mining must have caused considerable deforestation (Plate3.1. A photograph of wood stacks at the Copper Queen power plant around 1930 illustrates the quantity of fuel consumed, and a photograph (Plate 3.2) taken on Christmas Pass of traction engines hauling timber to Penhalonga and Rezende Mines shows the distance travelled to secure a supply of suitable wood in the late 19th/early 20th century. Forest has regenerated around the Copper Queen Mine because the area has been sparsely populated since earlier 20th century mining ceased. An aerial photo of the Rezende Mine (Plate 3.3) taken in 1975 shows woodland regeneration in the vicinity, perhaps because access was restricted by boundary fences, preventing firewood collection around the mine. Likewise an aerial photo of Simoona Hill (Plate 3. 4) taken in 1973 shows the open woodland canopy in stark contrast to

Plate 3.1: *An early view of Penhalonga and Rezende Mines*

Plate3. 2: *Traction engines hauling timber to Penhalonga and Rezende mines*

Plate 3.3: *Aerial view of Rezende Mines taken in 1975 (Scale 1: 6250).*

Plate 3.4: *Aerial view of Simoona Hill taken in 1973 (Scale 1: 12500)*

neighbouring cultivated areas, although numerous gold workings on the hill, both in prehistory and in colonial times (Tyndale-Biscoe 1933; Hoste 1977), must have stripped the hill of some of its woodland cover in the past. In areas of continued human settlement, the impact of firewood collection and field clearance would in most cases mask earlier causes of deforestation. If detailed studies of satellite images could differentiate between areas of primary and secondary growth then previously deforested areas which have since recovered could presumably be identified.

CONCLUSION

The quantity of charcoal required for manufacturing iron and copper products must have been substantial and should be taken into consideration in archaeological studies which examine environmental change. The use of remote sensing to study environmental degradation around areas of pre-20th century mining and metallurgy has been considered as a potential approach to this question. Ethnographic models and interdisciplinary studies of buried, datable material such as slag deposits, charcoal and pollen would probably prove useful. Initially field surveys are important to establish the spatial and chronological distribution of furnace types and production levels. Studies of the scale of iron production associated with complex societies, the potential environmental impact and consequent human responses could follow.

REFERENCES

Beach, D. (1977)
    "The Shona Economy: Branches of Production." In Palmer, R. & Parsons, N. (eds), *Roots of Rural Poverty*, 37-65. London: Heinemann.
Bisson, M. (1974)
    "Prehistoric Copper Mining in Northwestern Zambia." *Archaeology* 27(4): 242-247.
Carrion, J.S. (1992a)
    "Late Quaternary Pollen Sequence from Carihuela Cave, Southeastern Spain." *Review of Palaeobotany and Palynology* 71: 37-77.
Carrion, J.S. (1992b)
    "A Palaeoecological Study in the Western Mediterranean Area. The Upper Pleistocene Pollen Record from Cova Beneito (Alicante, Spain)." *Palaeogeography, Palaeoclimatology, Palaeoecology* 92: 1-14.

Carrion, J.S., Dupre, M., Fumanal, M.P. & Montes, R. (1995)
"A Palaeoenvironmental Study in Semi-arid Southeastern Spain: The Polynological and Sedimentological Sequence at Perneras Cave (Lorca, Murcia)." *Journal of Archaeological Science* 22: 355-367.

Chigwerewe, S.K. (1996)
"The Ecology and Management Potentials of Naturally Regenerated Teak Forests of the Kalahari-Namib Sandstone Formations in Zimbabwe." In Mushove, P.T., Shumba, E.M. & Matose, F. (eds), *Sustainable Management of Indigenous Forests in the Dry Tropics*. Harare, the Forest Commission: 148-154.

Cline, W. (1937)
Mining and Metallurgy in Negro Africa. General Series in Anthropology 5. Menasha: George Banta.

Collett, D. (1985)
"The Spread of Early Iron-using Communities in Eastern and Southern Africa." Unpublished *PhD* thesis, Cambridge.

de Barros, P. (1986)
"Bassar: a Quantified, Chronologically Controlled, Regional Approach to a Traditional Iron Production Centre in West Africa." *Africa*, 56 (2): 148-173.

Friede, H. (1983)
"Traditional Charcoal Burning in Southern Africa." *South African Archaeological Society Newsletter* 6 (2): 3.

Garlake, P.S. (1970
"The Decline of Zimbabwe in the Fifteenth Century." *Rhodesian Prehistory* 5: 6-8.

Garlake, P.S. (1971)
"An Iron Age Site on the Mukwichi River, Urungwe." *The South African Archaeological Bulletin* 26 (103 & 104): 147-152.

Goldsmith, B. & Carter, D.T. (1981)
The Indigenous Timbers of Zimbabwe. The Zimbabwe Bulletin of Forestry Research 9. Harare, the Forest Commission.

Gordon, R.B. & Killick, D.J. (1993)
"Adaptation of Technology to Culture and Environment: Bloomery Iron Smelting in America and Africa." *Technology and Culture* 34 (2): 243-270.

Goucher, C.L. (1981)
"Iron is Iron 'til it is Rust: Trade and Ecology in the Decline of West African Iron-smelting." *Journal of African History*, 22 (2): 179-189.

Haaland, R. (1980)
"Man's Role in the Changing Habitat of Mema During the Old Kingdom of Ghana." *Norwegian Archaeological Review*, 13 (1): 31-46.

Haaland, R. (1985)
"Iron Production, its Socio-cultural Context and Ecological Implications. In Haaland, R. & Shinnie, P. (eds), *African Iron Working: Ancient and Traditional*, 50-72. Bergen: Norwegian University Press.

Herbert, E.W. (1984)
Red Gold of Africa: Copper in Pre-colonial History and Culture. Madison: University of Wisconsin Press.

Herbert, E.W. (1996)
   "Metals and Power at Great Zimbabwe." In Pwiti, G. & Soper, R. (eds), *Aspects of African Archaeology*, 641-647. Harare: University of Zimbabwe Publications.
Hobley, C.W. (1922)
   Bantu Beliefs and Magic. London: Witherby.
Hoste, S. (1977)
   Gold Fever. Salisbury: Pioneer Head.
Huffman, T.N. (1977)
   "Zimbabwe: Southern Africa's First Town." *Rhodesian Prehistory* 7 (15): 9-14.
Huffman, T.N. (1996)
   "Archaeological Evidence for Climatic Change During the Last 2000 Years in Southern Africa." *Quaternary International* 33: 55-60.
Huffman, T.N. (2000)
   "Mapungubwe and the Origins of the Zimbabwe Culture." *The South African Archaeological Society: Goodwin Series* 8: 14-29.
Lane, P., Mapunda, B.B.B. & Eriksson, M. (2001)
   "Soil Erosion, Iron Smelting and Human Settlement in the Haubi Basin, North-central Tanzania." *Antiquity* 75: 803-804.
Mackenzie, J. (1974)
   "Furnace and Bellows Types in Iron Age Archaeology." *Rhodesian Prehistory*, 6 (13): 21-22.
Mackenzie, J.M. (1975)
   "A Pre-colonial Industry: The Njanja and the Iron Trade." *NADA* 11 (2): 200-220.
Maggs, T. (1982)
   "Mabhija: Pre-colonial Industrial Development in the Tugela Basin." *Annals of the Natal Museum*, 25 (1): 123-141.
Manyanga, M. (2000)
   "Choices and Constraints: Animal Resource Exploitation in South-eastern Zimbabwe c. AD 900-1500." *Studies in African Archaeology* 18. Uppsala: *Societas Archaeologica Uppsaliensis*.
Mihalyi, L.J. (1972)
   "Charcoal from the Zambian Forests." *Geographical Magazine*, 45(3): 212-218.
Miller, D. (1997)
   "Ironworking Technology." In Vogel, J.O. (ed) *Encyclopedia of Pre-colonial Africa*, Walnut Creek: Altamira Press, 132-135.
Ndoro, W. 1994
   "Natural-Draught Furnaces South of the Zambezi River." *Zimbabwean Prehistory*, (21): 29-32.
Pikirayi, I. (2001)
   The Zimbabwe Culture: Origins and Decline in Southern Zambezian States. Walnut Creek: Altamira Press.
Prendergast, M.D. (1972)
   "Pre-industrial Methods of Iron-smelting in Selected Tribal Trust Lands in Selukwe District, Rhodesia." Unpublished Report, Museum of Human Sciences Library.

Prendergast, M.D. (1974)
"Research into the Ferrous Metallurgy of Rhodesian Iron Age Societies." *Journal of the South African Institute of Mining and Metallurgy*, 74 (6): 254-264.

Prendergast, M.D. (1975)
A New Furnace Type from the Darwendale Dam Basin. *Rhodesian Prehistory*, 7(14): 16-20.

Prendergast, M.D. (1977)
"Stone-reinforced Furnaces from Masembura Tribal Trust Land, Rhodesia." *Rhodesian Prehistory* 7 (15): 17-18.

Prendergast, M.D. (1978)
"Two Nineteenth-century Metallurgical Sites in the Wedza and Gwelo Districts, Rhodesia." *Rhodesian Prehistory* (16): 11-17.

Prendergast, M.D. (1979a)
"Iron Age Settlements and Economy in Part of the Southern Zambezian Highveld." *The South African Archaeological Bulletin*, 34 (130): 111-119.

Prendergast, M.D. (1979b)
"Chisvingo Hill Furnace Site, Northern Mashonaland." In van der Merwe, N.J. & Huffman, T.N. (eds), *Iron Age Studies in Southern Africa*: Cape Town, South African Archaeological Society; Godwin Series No. 3: 47-51.

Prendergast, M.D. (1983)
"Early Iron Age Furnaces at Surtic Farm, Near Mazowe, Zimbabwe." *The South African Archaeological Bulletin*, 38 (137): 31-32.

Pwiti, G. (2001)
"Global Perspective Project Proposal - Africa." Unpublished Report, University of Zimbabwe.

Robinson, K.R. (1953)
"An Early Iron Smelting Site Near Khami Ruins, Matabeleland, Southern Rhodesia." *Occasional Paper of the National Museums of Southern Rhodesia* 2 (18): 508-517.

Schmidt, P.R. (1997a)
"Archaeological Views on a History of Landscape Change in East Africa." *Journal of African History* 38 (3): 393-421.

Schmidt, P.R. (1997b)
Iron Technology in East Africa. Oxford: James Currey.

Scoones, I. (1999)
"New Ecology and the Social Sciences: What Prospects for a Fruitful Engagement?" *Annual Review of Anthropology*, 28: 479-507.

Scott, L. & Brink, J.S. (1992)
"Quaternary Palaeoenvironments of Pans in Central South Africa: Palynological and Palaeontological Evidence." *South African Geographer* 19: 22-34.

Scott, L. (1996)
"Palynology of Hyrax Middens: 2000 Years of Palaeoenvironmental History in Namibia." *Quaternary International* 33: 73-79.

Shackleton, C.M. & Prins, F. (1993)
"Charcoal Yields from Dry Wood Samples of Ten Savanna Trees." *South African Archaeological Bulletin* 48: 42-44.

Summers, R. (1969)
"Ancient Mining in Rhodesia and Adjacent Areas." Museum Memoir (3). Salisbury: National Museums of Rhodesia.

Swan, L. (1994)
"Early Gold Mining on the Zimbabwean Plateau." *Studies in African Archaeology* 9. Uppsala: Societas Archaeologica Upsaliensis.

Swan, L.M. (1997)
"Salvage Excavation of an Iron-smelting Furnace Near Arcturus, Northern Zimbabwe." *Zimbabwea*, (5): 72-78.

Swan, L. (2002)
"Excavations at Copper Queen Mine, Northwestern Zimbabwe. "*South African Archaeological Bulletin,* 57 (176): 64-79.

Taylor, D. & Marchant, R. (1995)
"Human Impact in the Interlacustrine Region: Long-term Pollen Records from the Rukiga Highlands." *Azania* 29-30: 283-295.

Tessman, G. (1913)
Die Pangwe. Berlin: Ernst Wasmuth.

Tomlinson, R.W. (1973)
The Inyanga Area: An Essay in Regional Biogeography. University of Rhodesia, Series in Science, Occasional Paper 1.

Tylecote, R.F., Austin, J.N. & Wraith, A.E. (1971)
"The Mechanism of the Bloomery Process in Shaft Furnaces." *Journal of the Iron and Steel Institute* 209: 342-363.

Tyndale-Biscoe, R. (1933)
The Geology of the Central Part of the Mazoe Valley Gold Belt. Salisbury, Southern Rhodesia Geological Survey Bulletin No. 22.

van der Merwe, N.J. (1978)
"Field Methodology and Iron Age Metallurgy at Buhwa, Rhodesia." *Occasional Papers of the National Museums and Monuments of Rhodesia, Series A* 4 (3): 101-105.

van der Merwe, N.J. & Avery, D.H. (1987)
"Science and Magic in African Technology: Traditional Iron Smelting in Malawi." *Africa* 57 (2): 143-172.

Vogel, J.O. (1990)
"The Cultural Basis, Develoment and Consequences of a Socially Mediated Trading Corporation in Southern Zambezia." *Journal of Anthropological Archaeology* 9: 105-147.

Weeks, J.H. (1913)
Among Congo Cannibals. Philadelphia: Lippincott.

Wainwright, G.A. (1945)
"Iron in the Napatan and Meroitic Ages." *Sudan Notes and Records,* 26:5-36.

The Archaeology of Muleba, South West of Lake Nyanza: A Preliminary Report

4

Amandus Kwekason and Felix A. Chami

INTRODUCTION

This work is a preliminary report of the archaeological field work conducted in the district of Muleba, Kagera Region of Tanzania (Fig. 4.1) on the south-west part of Lake Nyanza. Apart from field school training, another purpose was to launch an archaeological project on the Tanzanian part of Lake Nyanza to complement similar efforts already launched on the Ugandan side by a newly initiated project called the African Archaeology Programme.

The decision to work in Muleba was the result of a report by a resident, a retired Tanzanian Cultural Officer, Mr. Peter Kalugira, about several rock shelters. His pictures indicated that the paintings were similar to those which had been documented by Chaplin (1974) from the rest of the lake region. The second author travelled to the district in April 2002 to confirm the reports and also to conduct a feasibility study. It was found that there were many rock shelters and rock hangings which had geometrical and non-naturalist paintings and within their surroundings pottery of Early Iron Working (EIW) were scattered.

RESEARCH PROBLEMS

It has been observed from virtually all archaeological reports from the Great Lakes Region that no excavated sites have been found to have a complete sequence covering the last 5000 years. Excavations like that of Chapman (1967) at Kansyore Island, on the Kagera River, had found cultural materials of the Late Stone Age (LSA), Early Iron Working (EIW) and later traditions in a disturbed context. Peter Schmidt (1997) who worked 50 km north of Muleba and Van Norten (1968) in Rwanda and Burundi concentrated on sites of the EIW period. Soper and Golden (1969) excavated on the southern part of the Lakes Region, around Mwanza, and reported on cultural materials ranging from the Early Stone Age to recent times. However, these were in a disturbed context. The same picture was reported by Collett and Robertshaw (1980) from the Gogo Falls of the Kenyan Nyanza. However, the fieldwork to re-examine the Gogo Falls site by Robertshaw (1991) yielded sections with a sequence at least for the LSA and EIW period.

Another problem is theoretical in relation to the question of rock painting done in red ochre and in a few cases in orange/yellow paint. Whereas non-naturalistic and geometric paintings have been observed in many parts of eastern and central Africa, between Zambia and north-east Africa, there is no consensus about the period of their production and the nature of the population responsible for them. Chaplin (1967) who has discussed these types of paintings, probably more exhaustively than anyone, has presented different positions as to who executed them and when. Those rock paintings have either been attributed to LSA people (Khoisan speakers) or Iron-using people (Bantu speakers) or "Hima" pastoralists alleged to have invaded the Great Lakes Region either in about the 15th century (see Chaplin 1974; Soper and Golden 1969) or in about the 12th century (Grunderbeek 1981: 27). Soper and Golden (1969) have attributed the geometric paintings to the LSA people and the paintings displaying objects like hoes to EIW people. It should also be noted that Phillipson's (1976) study of similar rock paintings from eastern Zambia attributed some of them to the EIW people.

Muleba Environment

The geographical position of the Muleba District is shown on Figure 4.1. The islands of Bumbire and Iramba are included. The environment of the general area of the western part of Lake Nyanza, including geology, soils, weather, biomass, and various subsistence activities, has been well described by Schmidt

(1978). Following his description, Muleba falls between latitude 1° S and 2° S and within the 10 km width from the lake of the mostly settled landscape. However, the district extends further west to the area with hills, escarpments and marshes forming the catchments of River Ngono, which flows northward parallel with the lake shore to empty into Kagera River. The population concentration in the hinterland of Muleba is on the hill tops and slopes. The settlements here seem to have continued from the LSA. As Schmidt (1978, 1997) has shown, the vegetation here is not primary as clearance for cultivation and other purposes has continued from the beginning of the early farming communities

The topography of this landscape from the lake shore to about 20 km in the interior is made up of two main escarpments, the first one rising abruptly from the lake for about 150 meters with only a few gently sloping shelves of not more than 100 meters wide. It is this part of the shoreline that has a population concentrating on fishing and trading. Banana groves are also found there. The rocky escarpment has rock hangings and shelters which seem to have been occupied in the past. After the first escarpment the landscape is generally flat, being interrupted by ravines made up of streams and marshes which feed into Ngono River. Muleba town is located on part of this flat landscape between 5-6 km from the lake. Another major valley through which holds Ngono River runs, is encountered about 10 km from the lake flanked on the western side by a high rising escarpment giving way to a set of hilly landscape. The population concentrations of Rubya and Nshamba are found on these hills. Banana growing and cattle keeping are the main agricultural activities. On the escarpments are many caves, rock shelters and hangings dominated by red paintings mentioned earlier. The dominant rock of this area is sandstone and the soils are derived from its weathering process (Schmidt 1978: 20).

The area of Muleba also seems to receive less rain than the northern part of the lake around Bukoba town, falling a little bit below the 1,250 millimetres of the normal precipitations near the shore (see Schmidt 1978: 12, 26). Indeed the landscape is more savanna compared with the area north of the district.

Fieldwork

The fieldwork consisted of three stages; field survey to find sites and establish

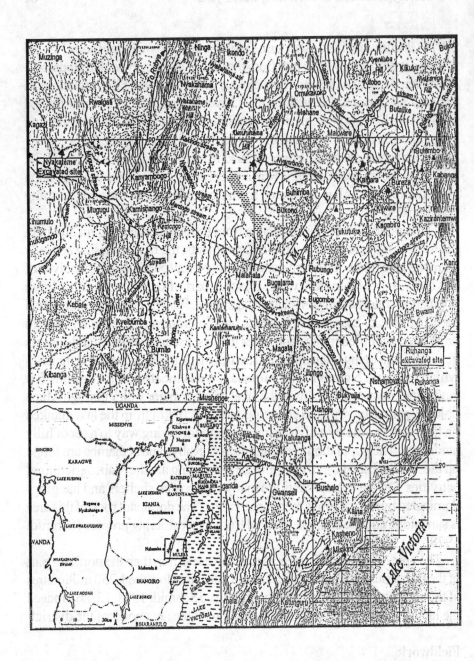

Figure 4.1: *Map of Muleba District in Kagera Region* (Insert map see, Schmidt 1997)

patterns of settlement around the district, excavation of selected sites and recording of rock paintings. Survey work lasted two weeks and excavation and the recording of rock paintings lasted for four weeks.

Survey

The purpose of the survey work was to use the town of Muleba as a centre, survey all directions east as far as the near shore islands in the lake, the interior to about 20 km and survey about 5 km north and south of the town.

From the base at Muleba town, the first survey efforts were directed to the area north-west of the town. The purpose was to explore the gently sloping landscape towards the valley of River Ngono. A site, located south of a small hill called Omuruhama (see Fig. 4.1), with a concentration of pottery of rouletted tradition was found after crossing a swamp before entering River Ngono. Another effort was directed southwards along the main road to Biharamulo. No site was observed as far as River Kabukunja about 2 km from the town. The survey was then directed to the hill slopes following the river to the east. Potsherds of a time range from the EIW to the rouletted traditions were seen scattered on a long span of land with no particular concentration. The survey extended 2 km from the river bridge.

From Muleba to the north-east following the road to Bukoba a series of surveys were conducted for about 5 km to Butembo. A concentration of EIW potsherds was observed at about 1km, on a sloping landscape, west of Butembo Primary School. Near the valley in the same area is a large cave with no archaeological material inside. However, a concentration of pottery of early traditions was observed in the area around the cave. A scatter of similar pottery was found east of Butembo close to the margin of the escarpment dropping down to the lake. A large site, with a concentration of rouletted pottery, was also found south of the school on the path going to Kazirantema village. In the same place pottery was also observed of post AD 1700, related to the 17th-19th century trade network. Further south, from Butembo, following the cultivated landscape along the cliff margin, rather than the main road, at the village of Bureza was found another concentration of rouletted ware.

Another survey effort concentrated on the west, along the road to Rubya and Nshamba. It was noted earlier that the escarpments on this side have many rock hangings and shelters. A recent site, discussed earlier as of post AD 1700, was found in the village after crossing the bridge of River Ngono. After the junction of Rubia and Nshamba road on the escarpment on the right side of River Nyakateme a concentration of pottery of EIW tradition was observed. Some of this pottery scatter occurs near rock shelters of which seven were surveyed and recorded. A number of slags were also seen associated with the pottery suggesting smelting in the area.

Another effort was to survey the flat area south-east of the Muleba town, along the escarpment between Ruhanga and Katunguru, following the flat land along the lake escarpment to the shore settlements of Ruhanga and Katunguru. The survey also discovered a rock shelter at the higher part of the escarpment, on the path climbing down to Ruhanga overlooking the lake. At Butalimwa village, before climbing down the escarpment to the shore village of Misikiro, a Late Stone Age (LSA) site with lithics and pottery, preliminarily identified as of Kansyore tradition and later traditions including EIW and rouletted traditions were found. At Misikiro village at the shore shelf much pottery of roulette and recent potsherds were observed.

The last survey effort was on the islands of Iramba and Kibumba. We hired motor boats from Ruhanga and had about 5 hours of survey on Iramba Island. The area is an archipelago naturally arranged in such a manner that a calm bay occurs between the islands with several entrances from north-east, south and west. The population is concentrated on the islands' side of the bay. They are mainly fishing communities with very little or no agriculture since the islands are all rocky. On top of Iramba Island, where a layer of soil is found, was observed many potsherds of Kansyore and EIW traditions. Other later traditions were observed at the lower part of the island where the modern population resides.

Excavation

Several sites were earmarked for excavation, both open air and rock shelter sites. Of the most interesting open air sites was the Butalemwa and Iramba Island site. It was thought that their excavations would be reminiscent of other open air sites excavated around the lake and found disturbed. Four rock shelter sites were found interesting for excavation: three from Nyakateme near the road to Nshamba and the Ruhanga site on the higher part of the escarpment facing the lake. The decision arrived at was to focus on rock shelters for two reasons: firstly, it was likely that they would not have been disturbed and hence they could assist in offering a long cultural sequence and second, their excavation could also shed some light on the question of rock paintings.

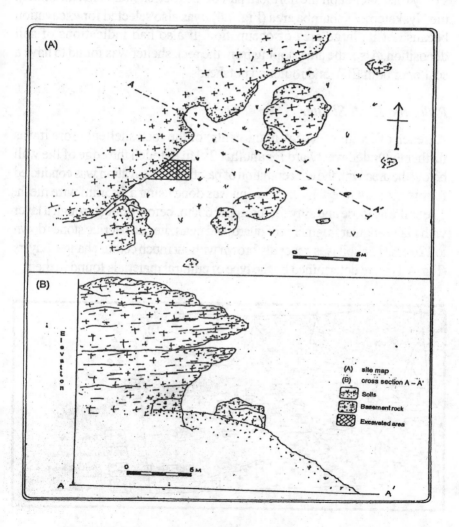

Figure 4.2: *Ruhanga site map indicating the profile of the rock shelter.*

The rock shelter overlooking lake Ruhanga (Fig. 4.2) was selected for excavation because it was the only rock painting site found near the lake. It was assumed that the occupants performed some activities to do with the lake, probably including fishing, and data from this shelter would be compared with that obtained from other rock shelters 15 km away from the lake. A storey rock shelter on the northern part of the rock shelter concentration in the Nyakateme/Nshamba area (Fig. 4.4), was also selected for excavation because of its large area of occupation. It also had indications of soil deposition. Also, the area sloping from the rock shelter was found to have a scatter of both EIW and rouletted potsherds.

Ruhanga Rock Shelter

A trench of 1x2m was sunk at the centre of the rock shelter before it was further extended westward for another 2x1m to touch the edge of the wall below the area with the concentration of paintings. Excavation was conducted following 5 cm intervals and sieving was done using a 5x5mm wire mesh. The soil was loose and silty for the upper 60cm, before going through a layer with many angular fragments of quartz and quartzite and lateritic stones down to 120 cm. The soil was generally brown without much colour change. Layers (Fig. 4.3) were determined by the type of cultural materials found in them.

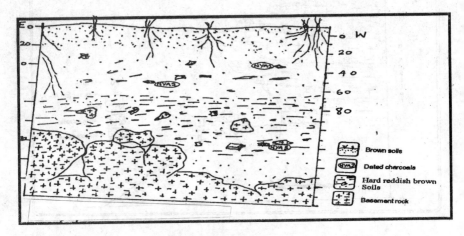

Fig. 4.3: *Stratigraphy of Ruhanga rock shelter*

The first 10 centimetres were sterile suggesting that no recent occupation has taken place in the shelter. It was from 10 cm down to 30 cm that pottery of rouletted tradition of knotted-strip technique was recovered (see Soper 1985; Plate 4.4a). From thereon down to 75 cm were recovered potsherds of EIW tradition. An iron point was recovered between 65 and 70 cm. Between 50 and 75 cm were encountered a few potsherds of Kansyore tradition (Plate 4.2) and a sizable amount of microliths. Both categories of artifacts continued down to 85-90 cm. After that, lithics artifacts of the MSA became. dominant. These were characterised by points, cores, scrappers and blades Plate 4.1).

Another important class of artifacts found were lateritic stones associated with red ochre fragments from 35 cm down to about 80cm. Several large, used red-ochre pencils (Plate 4.4b) were recovered suggesting that they were used by EIW and Kansyore occupants to paint the wall. Fragments of bones of animals and burnt tree seeds yet to be identified were also found especially in the EIW/Kansyore context as well as grinding stones. Charcoal samples were collected from all the levels with cultural materials above 100 cm. Four of them have been submitted for analysis, from level 95 cm, 65 cm, 45cm and 20cm. Sample Gr A-22028 collected just below 90 cm the last level to yield Kansyore pottery dates BP 240 $\pm$ 40 (414 BC). Several other samples have dated the roulette tradition to between AD 1040 to AD 1667.

Nyakateme Rock Shelter

At this site (Fig. 4.4) similar excavation methods were used following five cm intervals. The soil here was more compact, being more clay and some parts were disturbed by ants. The soil is brownish becoming more reddish towards the bottom. The first 40 cm yielded pottery of the rouletted tradition mainly of faint knotted strip roulettes and of a cord string roulette. No typical elaborated knotted string roulette potsherds were found in the excavation at Nyakateme. However, they were found on the surface on the land sloping from the cave suggesting that the tradition was also represented. Between 50 and 100 cm were recovered potsherds of EIW tradition.

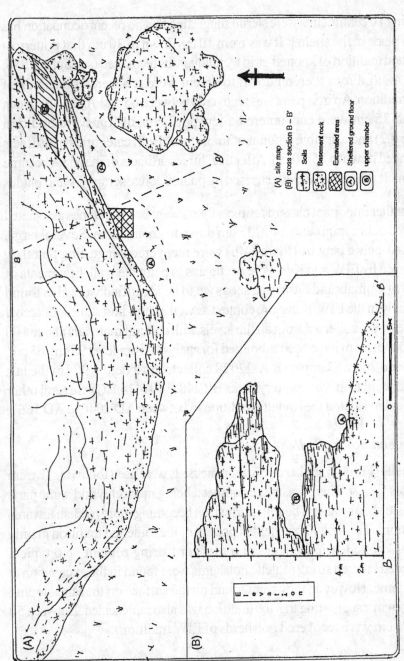

Figure 4. 4: *Nyakete site map with the profile of the rock shelter*

Table 4. 1: *Muleba excavation report -Ruhanga site*

Trench	Level	Depth	Pottery Ks	EIW	T/R	Roll	OE	Slags	Metal	Lithics	Ochre	Painted stone	Bones	Seeds	Charcoal	Remarks
1	1-2	0-10	-	-	-	-	-	-	-	-	-	-	-	-	-	Sterile
1	3	10-15	-	-	2	5		-							1	
1	4	15-20	-	-	2		5	-	-			-	-	-	3	
1	5	20-25			1		4							1	2	
1	6	25-30					1							1	2	
1	7	30-35					4								2	
1	8	35-40	-		1		4	-	-		1	-	1	1	1	
1	9	40-45	-		5		8	-	-		2	-	1	2	5	
1	10	45-50	3		2		5				2			1	2	
1	11	50-55	2		2		13			12	5				2	
1	12	55-60	4				6			67	10	-			1	
1	13	60-65	7				14			76	16		1	2	2	
1	14	65-70	7	4			17		1	97	17		2	3	2	
1	15	70-75	9	1			4			96	5		1	1	1	
1	16	75-80		2			2			175	3		2	2	1	
1	17	80-85								80	1		2	2	1	
1	18	85-90	2							15	1		1		-	
1	19	90-95	-							25						
1	20	95-100								15						
1	21	100-105	-	-			-	-	-	75	-		-	-	1	
1	22	105-110	-	-			-	-	-	24	-		-	-	-	
1	23	110 -								15					-	Scraper

Key: Ks = Kansyore, EIW = Early Iron Working, T/R = Twisted Roulette, Roll = Roulette, OE = Other pottery

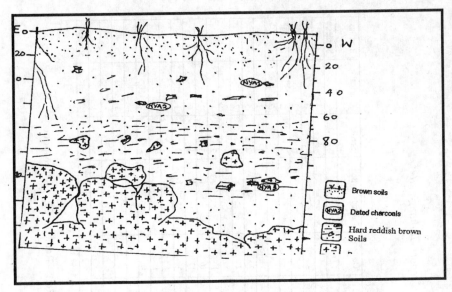

Fig. 4.5: *Stratigraphy of Nyakateme rock shelter*

Other artefacts recovered include lithics from about 90 cm, with no geometric tools but microliths, a few red ochre fragments, and many exfoliated rock fragments those in layer 55-60cm having red colour suggesting that the red colour painting had been done at least before the introduction of rouletted ware tradition. A charcoal sample Pta 8828 collected from level 50-55, the lowest level to yield rouletted pottery offered a date of BP 590 ± 45 (AD 1326). No exfoliated stone pieces were recovered with the orange/yellow colour suggesting that this kind of painting could have been done after the EIW period. EIW tradition is dated by charcoal sample Pta 8826 of BP 1710 ± 50 (AD 339). A few animal bone fragments were also recovered.

DISCUSSION

Since this is a preliminary report, the discussion should be limited to the range of finds in relation to the problems stated above. As suggested earlier, aspects of discussion include the question of chronology and rock painting. The survey work has shown that the area of Muleba was intensively settled from the LSA to the modern day. Sites representing different cultural

Table 4. 2: *Muleba excavation report-Nyakateme site*

Trench	Level	Depth CM	Ks	EIW	K/R	Roll	OE	Slag	Metal	Lithics	Ochre	Painted stone	Bones	Seeds	Charcoal	Remarks
1	3	10-15					4							1		
1	4	15-20					10								1	
1	5	20-25				1	16				2					
1E	5-6	20-30					14									
1	7	30-35				1	3								1	
1E	7-8	30-40				2	19								1	
1	8	35-40					2									
1	9	40-45					11									
1E	9-10	40-50					37		3						1	Iron
1	10	45-50					15					6				
1	11	50-55		1			12				1				1	
1E	11-12	50-60		2			6								1	
1	12	55-60					7					3	8			
1	13	60-65		3			7									
1E	13-14	60-70					3									
1	14	65-70					11								1	
1	15	70-75					21								1	
1E	15-16	70-80					1									
1	16	75-80		4			18				1				1	
1	17	80-85					9								1	
1E	17-18	80-90					5			1						
1	18	85-90		1			13								1	
1	19	90-95					3									
1E	19-20	90-100		1			2			2					1	
1	20	95-100					3			4					1	
1	21	100-105					8			4	2				1	
1E	21	100-105	1	1						20					1	
1	22	105-110								10	3				1	
1	23	110-115								14	4				2	
1	24	115-120	2				1			8	2					
1	25	120-150														

Key: Ks = Kansyore, EIW = Early Iron Working, T/R = Twisted Roulette, Roll = Roulette, OE = Other pottery occupations, some being of multiple occupation were found in different parts of Muleba. These findings are not new for the Great Lakes Region. It has been shown for the Mwanza region (Soper and Golden 1969) and for the Nyanza part of Kenya (Collett and Robertshaw 1980) and for parts of Uganda (Chapman 1967; Robertshaw 2000; Connah 1996; Reid 1990) and Rwanda/Burundi (Van Noten 1979; Van Grunderbeek 1981) that similar sites have been found. Of significance from our research was the excavation of the undisturbed rock shelters which were expected to offer samples for dating for the different horizons in the cultural sequence.

It would seem that before the development of the ceramic LSA tradition, Kansyore, now dated to between 4000-500 BC (Chapman 1968; Collett and Robertshaw 1980; Mehleman 1977; Bower and Nelson 1978; Bower 1978), there existed a pre-ceramic LSA culture, having its technology derived from the MSA traditions. The find of the stone assemblage (Plate 4.1) of this earlier tradition below 90cm of the Ruhanga rock shelter would probably be the first incontrovertible evidence for this tradition around the lake. This non-ceramic LSA tradition dates before 500 BC as shown by our sample GrA A-22028. The find of these cultural materials in a rock shelter facing the lake may also suggest that pre-Kansyore LSA people had also exploited lacustrine resources.

The two rock shelters yielded pottery of the Kansyore tradition similar to Chapman's (1967: Fig. 7c and Fig.10). Robertshaw (1991) has Oltome as a synonym for Kansyore. These are potsherds with parallel lines and sometimes with horizontal and vertical band on one sherd intersecting (Plate 4. 2). Another type of decoration is of parallel rows of closely spaced dots on potsherds from a vessel made by a coil technique (Plate 4. 2). The breakage of the pottery has followed this weak coiling line. The variety of other types of decoration is provided by Chapman from the site of Kansyore. In the discussion about the Kansyore pottery traditions, a pattern has emerged suggesting that the tradition emerged first in the Rift valley of Tanzania and Kenya before being adopted in the Lakes Region in the last millennium BC (see Mehlman 1977; Bower and Nelson 1978; Collect and Robertshaw 1980). It would seem that there was a widespread aceramic/Neolithic tradition of early farmers and of cattle keepers covering the area from the Sudan to the rest of east and probably southern Africa (for conspectus see Chami and Kwekason 2003). Indeed, Chapman (1967: 177; see also Phillipson 1993) was of the opinion that there is a similarity between Kansyore Ware and the early Sudan pottery. Collett and Robertshaw (1980) have refuted that argument. Kansyore pottery is also found in the area around Nguru Hills close to the Tanzanian coast (Thorp 1992).

However, whereas the presence of Kansyore tradition in the Kenya Rift Valley has been denied by Collett and Robertshaw (1980), Bower and Nelson (1978, also Bower 1978) have strongly acknowledged it. They agree that this tradition occurs at the earliest levels of the Pastoral Neolithic mainly in association with material of the Nderit tradition. The early dates for the Kansyore tradition in the Rift Valley in association with pottery of Nderit may suggest that the two were the same and became diversified at a later stage as the Rift Valley was mainly Narosura and the Great Lakes Region continued to remain Kansyore. Collett and Robertshaw (1980) are of the opinion that further study of the Pastoral Neolithic traditions is required to solve this problem.

Furthermore, scholars studying the Pastoral Neolithic tradition in the region have viewed the people of the Kansyore tradition in the Great Lakes Region as not having practised domestication of plants and animals due to the lack of evidence for domesticates from excavated sites. It should be noted here that in the absence of remains of domesticates other cultural materials have been used to suggest agriculture including grinding stones, stone bowls and pestle rubbers (Sutton 1973; Ordner 1972).

The absence of bones of domesticated animals in our excavations would continue to support the assumption that the Kansyore people did not practise agriculture. However, the rock art data discussed below and the presence for cattle in the economy of Kansyore in the Rift Valley would call for re-examination of this evidence. On the other hand, the finds of grinding stones could also be used to hypothesise agriculture: it is possible that they were used for processing wild cereals. We would argue here that since agriculture has been attributed to the EIW people without much material evidence it would not be logical to discount domestication by the Kansyore people. Indeed some evidence has been recovered in Cameroon showing that such people had already domesticated banana (Mbida 2000). Ehret (1998; also

Plate 4.1: *MSA derived lithics from Ruhanga Rock Shelter*

Plate 4. 2: *Kansyore wares from Muleba*

Plate 4.3: *EIW pottery tradition from Muleba*

Plate 4. 4: (a) *Rouletted pottery tradition from Muleba*
(b) *Orchre materials for mural painting*

Plate 4.5: *Rock paintings of Muleba*

Schoenbrun 1993) has stressed the point that the Great Lakes Region was settled by people of Sahelian origin domesticating animals/ plants and smelting iron before the alleged Bantu speakers' immigration (see Chami 2001 for criticism). He has put this transitional period from between1000-500 BC. Ehret does not indicate whether the Sahelians were the same people making Kansyore tradition whose pottery was suggested to be similar to that of the Sudan. As shown above, Kansyore tradition at Muleba dates after 500 BC only a century or two before the EIW tradition is introduced.

There is much more information available about the economy and technology of the EIW traditions (Schmidt 1978; 1997; Schoenbrun 1993). Our excavated ceramics (Plate 3) may be able to provide at least two tentative phases of this tradition. It has been shown elsewhere (Chami 1998) that the coastal EIW tradition which lasted for about six hundred years had three phases in its development. It is our hypothesis that a similar occurrence took place in the Great Lakes Region and it is just a matter of time before this is illustrated. It is logical that a tradition lasting about a thousand years would have gone through different phases in its development. Our opinion will be consolidated after analyses are complete.

The debate over whether the EIW tradition was spread by peoples' movements from Cameroon (see Phillipson 1993; Ehret 1998) or by other means has been presented elsewhere (see Gramly 1978; Chami 1999, 2001). What is being observed from both excavations is a layer of 15 centimetres where the Kansyore and EIW cultural materials are mixed, suggesting a transition and continuity or replacement of the former by the latter. The idea of continuity from the LSA to the EIW period (see Chami 1999, 2001, Chami and Kwekason 2003; Gramly 1978) has not been accepted by many scholars. Phillipson (1976) explained the mixture of LSA and EIW materials as cultures in exchange or contact. Robertshaw (1991) has proposed bioturbation and exchange and virtually all scholars discussing the emergence of the EIW tradition in the region have argued for replacement of population by the newcomers.

The period between 500 AD and 1000 AD has been a period of the missing link as no tradition has affirmatively been attributed to this period. According to Schmidt (1997: 19):

At this time we cannot say what happened to these populations, although there is
suggestive linguistic evidence that many of these .. people left the region and moved into
the area that we know today in the north as Ankole, western Buganda, and Bunyoro.

Robertshaw (1991: 67) observes that the EIW tradition was replaced by a
tradition with a variety of roulettes around 1000 AD without suggesting that
the EIW tradition continued up to then or that there was a hiatus between the
EIW and the rouletting traditions. However, Van Grunderbeek (1981: 28)
has shown that a rouletting tradition existed in Rwanda and Burundi in about
AD 750.

As has been shown on the Tanzania coast (Chami 1998) and on the
northern highlands of Tanzania (see Maro 2002) continuity occurred from
the EIW period to the later traditions. Realignment of settlements due to
environmental factors and change of trade routes could have occurred (see
Chami & Pikirayi: *this volume*). However, those traditions that emerged
after 500 AD continued to about 900 AD when they were replaced by other
later traditions which continued to the second millenium AD. It is logical that
a similar occurrence would have happened in the Great Lakes Region coupled
with possible migrations due to climate change of the mid-first millennium AD
(see Chami: *this volume*). However the two excavations suggest a missing
link between EIW and rouletted tradition. Our earliest date for rouletting
tradition is that of AD 1040, the date which supports the finds of Schmidt
(1997) and Robertshaw (1991). The missing link could have been caused
by climatic change (Chami: *this volume*)

The idea that the rouletting technique (Plate 4.4a) reached the region from
the Sahel in about the beginning of the first millennium AD has been suggested
by Connah (1996). Schmidt (1997) has argued that carved wood roulettes
anteceded the other types of roulettes in the early part of the second millennium
AD. Soper (1985) has shown that the technique had been used in Rwanda
from about the 8th and the 9th century AD. The probable early use of the
rouletting technique in East Africa is suggested by a potsherd found from the
hinterland of the coast of Tanzania dating from about 600-800 AD (Chami
1994:73) and those from Rwanda and Burundi dating from AD 750 (Van
Grunderbeek 1981). It would also seem that some pottery recovered from
the EIW context in the Ruhanga site had carved-wood roulettes as a lip

decoration. The point being made here is that rouletting as a technique of pottery decoration could have been used in the region of eastern Africa before its intensive use and diversification at about the end of the first millennium AD.

Apart from the chronological information used for the discussion above, the Muleba work recorded the rock paintings from several rock shelters (Plate 4.5). It was suggested earlier that several red ochre pencils (Plate 4.4) and lumps were found in the Ruhanga excavations in association with Kansyore and EIW traditions suggesting that the painting in red was done during that time. At the Nyakateme site, red painted exfoliated stone pieces were found in association with the EIW cultural tradition also supporting the point. The idea therefore that people of a Hima tradition, pastoralists, painted the rock shelters after a date of 15th century, as suggested by Chaplin (1967), is no longer sustained by the results of this research.

No single painting in this area was found to represent any naturalistic paintings of animals and human beings as found mainly in central Tanzania (see Leakey 1983) and southern Africa (Garlake 1987). All paintings are of what has been called geometric or impressionistic or simply non-naturalistic types found mainly in the rest of the Great Lakes Region (see Chaplin 1974) extending southward to eastern Zambia (Phillipson 1976). Such rock paintings can also be seen in the Eyasi Basin in the Tanzania Rift Valley, the horn of Africa (see Graziosi 1964) and southern tip of Arabia (see Bulletin of the Society for Arabian Studies 2007/7:43) including Sokotra Island (Naumkin and Sedov 1995) and southern Europe (see Anati 1964). The paintings at all rock shelters except those excavated at Nyakateme were done in red.

The most common painted motif is that of stick figures, called matchstick figures by Chaplin (1967) sometimes with no heads but neck, body, arms and legs. The figures sometimes have three pairs of limbs some bowed upward or downward and in some cases having a protuberance between the legs. Whereas Chaplin (1967) interpreted these as representing cattle, since some of the upper pairs of limbs seem to have been carved upward as horns and that similar representation of cattle appear in Ethiopia, Graziosi (1964) and Anati (1960) studying similar rock art in Ethiopia and southern Europe respectively have suggested that these are human schematic figures.

If some of the stick figures really represent cattle, according to Chaplin

(1967), that some of the upper limb-like extensions curving upward or downward are horns (Graziozi 1964: 97), then what it means is that the people of the Great Lakes Region had kept cattle probably from the time of Kansyore. This is further evidence against the Hima's responsibility for the rock painting. As noted earlier, the Hima are alleged to have arrived in the region at the earliest in the 12th century (Van Grunderbeek 1981). If the painting is an aspect of Hima culture then this means that the Bachwezi/Bahinda myth attributing domestication to a ruling dynasty, sometimes thought by scholars to be of non-Bantu speakers, existed in the region from the LSA period, in the last millennium BC or earlier, and not in the 12th-15th century (see the critique of the myth by Sutton 1990) . It should also be noted that Van Grunderbeek (1981: 27) reported of a bone of small cattle from a mid-first millennium AD context from Rwanda/Burundi arguing that cattle had been kept "before Batutsi arrival" in the 12th century. He has also cited Epistein who observed painted short-horned cattle around Mount Elgon not far from the Lakes. Probably the same is observed in Odak's (1977) report of red rock paintings with cattle from western Kenya. Schmidt (1997) has shown that some of the oral traditions, especially dealing with iron smelting, can be traced back to the EIW period. Excavations elsewhere have also shown that large sites attributed to the alleged Hima invaders date back to before the 15th century (Robertshaw 2000; Reid 1990).

Other mural illustrated motifs include rounded paintings representing what has commonly been know as sun (Leakey 1983), star motifs, circles with dots inside, circles divided in half, a snake motif, a form of letters E, A, and H, a figure like a hand or foot with fingers and a variety of irregular and regular box figures some having lines intersecting forming columns and rows. Looking at the combination of these motifs, especially from the rest of the Lake Region, Ethiopian, Sokotra and eastern Zambia, an hypothesis is advanced here suggesting that some of the paintings represent ancient writing system. This suggests that we need to change our thinking from focusing on rock paintings as mere art, ritualistic symbols and mere impressionistic figures and move forward to establish patterns of combination of these figures to launch a process of deciphering the literature if that will ever be possible.

CONCLUSION

The archaeology of the Muleba District has established a set of archaeological sites shedding further light on the prehistory of the Great Lakes Region. A sequence from the LSA to modern times has been established. The recording of the rock paintings and the findings of its features in archaeological excavations has shed light on the time period when the paintings were executed and the cultural tradition responsible for it. The future plan is to compare these findings with those to be collected by colleagues in Uganda in the African Archaeology Programme. Joint work with Ugandans with the purpose of understanding the cultural dynamics of the Lake Nyanza and the Uganda Nile is being planned and we hope future field efforts will shed even brighter light on the problems outlined earlier.

REFERENCES

Anati, E. (1964)
   Camonica Valley. London: Jonathan Cape.
Bower, J. (1973)
   "Seronera: Excavations at a Stone Bowl Site in the Serengeti National Park, Tanzania." *Azania* 8: 71-104.
Bower, J. (1986)
   "A Survey of Surveys: Aspects of Surface Archaeology in Sub-Saharan Africa." *African Archaeology Review* 4: 21-40.
Bower, J. and Nelson, C. (1978)
   "Early Pottery and Pastoral Cultures of the Central Rift Valley, Kenya." *Man* 13:554-66.
Chami, F. (1994)
   The Tanzanian Coast in the First Millennium AD. Studies in African Archaeology 7. Uppsala: Societas Archaeologica Upsaliensis.
Chami, F. (1998)
   "A Review of Swahili Archaeology." *African Archaeological Review* 15 (3): 99-218.
Chami, F. (1999)
   Graeco-Romans Trade Link and the Bantu Migration Theory. *Anthropos* 94 (1-3): 237-215.
Chami, F. (2001)
   "A Response to Christopher Ehret's 'Bantu Expansions.'" *International Journal of African Historical Studies* 34/3: 647-651.
Chami, F. and Kwekason, A. (2003)
   "Neolithic Pottery Traditions From the Islands, the Coast and the Interior of East Africa." *African Archaeological Review* 20 (2)
Chami, F. and Mapunda, B. (1996)
   "The 1996 Archaeological Reconnaissance North of the Rufiji Delta." *Nyame Akuma* 43: 38-45.

Chaplin, T. (1974)
 "The Prehistoric Rock Art of the Lake Victoria Region." *Azania* 9: 1-50.
Chapman, S. (1967)
 "Kansyore Island." *Azania* 2: 554-66.
Collett, D. and Robertshaw, P. (1980)
 "Early Iron Age and Kansyore Pottery: Finds From Gogo Falls, South Nyanza." *Azania* 15:
 133-145.
Connah, G. (1996)
 Kibiro: The Salt of Bunyoro, Past and Present. London: BIEA.
Ehret, C. (1998)
 An African Classical Age. Oxford: Oxford University Press.
Garlake, P. (1987)
 The Painted Caves. Harare: Palladio Press.
Gramly, R. (1978)
 "Expansion of Bantu-speakers versus Development of Bantu Language In Situ. An
 Archaeologist's Perspective." *South African Archaeological Bulletin* 33: 107-112.
Graziosi, P. (1964)
 "New Discoveries of Rock Paintings in Ethiopia." *Antiquity* 38: 91-98.
Grunderbeek, van M. (1981)
 The Iron Age in Rwanda and Burundi. *Nyame Akuma* 18:26-32.
Leakey, M. (1983)
 Africa's Vanishing Art: the Painting of Tanzania. New York: Doubleday and Comp.
Maro, E. (2002)
 "Cultural Continuity: Technological and Stylistic Evolution of Pottery in North Pare in the
 1st Millennium AD." *MA* Thesis: University of Dar-es-Salaam.
Mbida, C. *et al,* (2000)
 "Evidence for Banana Cultivation and Animal Husbandry During the First Millennium BC
 in the Forest of Southern Cameroon." *Journal of Archaeological Science* 27: 151-162.
Mehleman, M. (1977)
 "Excavations at Nasera Rock, Tanzania." *Azania* 12: 111-118.
Odak, Osaga (1977)
 "Kakapeli and Other Rock Paintings in Western Kenya." *Azania* 12:187-192.
Ordner, K (1972)
 "Narosura." *Azania* 7: 24-92.
Phillipson, D. (1976)
 The Prehistory of Eastern Zambia. Nairobi: British Institute in Eastern Zambia.
Phillipson, D. (1993)
 African Archaeology. Cambridge: Cambridge University Press.
Reid, A. (1990)
 "Ntusi and its Hinterland." *Nyame Akuma* 33: 26-8.
Robertshaw, P. (1991)
 "Gogo Falls: A Complex Site East of Lake Victoria." *Azania* 26: 63-196.
Robertshaw, P. (2000)
 "Climate Change and the Rise of Political Complexity in Western Uganda." *Journal of
 African History* 41: 1-28.

Schmidt, P. (1978)
   Historical Archeology. Westport: Greenwood Press
Schmidt, P. (1997)
   Iron Technology in East Africa. Bloomington: Indiana University Press.
Schoenbrun, D. (1993)
   "We are What We Eat: Ancient Agriculture Between the Great Lakes." *Journal of African History* 34: 1-31.
Soper, R. (1985)
   "Roulette Decoration on African Pottery: Technical Consideration, Dating and Distributions." *The African Archaeological Review* 3: 29-51.
Soper, R. and Golden, B. (1969)
   "Archeological Survey of Mwanza Region, Tanzania." *Azania* 4: 15-79.
Sutton, J. (1973)
   The Archaeology of the Western Highlands of Kenya. Nairobi: BIEA.
Sutton, J. (1990)
   A Thousand Years of East Africa. Nairobi: BIEA.
Thorp, C. (1992)
   "Archaeology in the Nguru Hills." *Azania* 27:21-44.
Van Noten, F. (1979)
   "The Early Iron Age in the Interlacustrine Region." *Azania* 14: 61-80.

Excavation of a Late Holocene Cave Deposit in the Southern Namib Desert

5

John Kinahan

INTRODUCTION

The southern Namib Desert forms a longitudinal dune sea extending northward from the lower Orange River in southwestern Africa. Broad gravel plains, representing ancient outwash fans, lie along the eastern margin of the dune sea, at the foot of a precipitous escarpment formed by the Huib-Hoch Plateau. Archaeological investigations in the highland zone have revealed a Holocene sequence with a hiatus of approximately 5,000 years, followed by re-occupation in the first millennium AD (Sievers 1984; Wendt 1972). It has been suggested that this gap in the sequence corresponds to a period of sparse occupation throughout southern Namibia (Vogel & Visser 1981).

Generally an inhospitable environment, the southern Namib receives an average of less than 100mm precipitation per year, mainly in the winter months. The vegetation of the desert responds rather prolifically to the rainfall, resulting in a flush of annual grass cover that is exploited by migratory antelope, including *Oryx gazella*, and a wide variety of other species such as ostrich *Struthio camelus*. In the past, such movements would have attracted hunter-gatherer communities to foray into the desert during the winter months. Until recently, however, no archaeological surveys had been conducted on the margins of the dune sea to the west of the escarpment in the southern Namib Desert.

81

The results of a series of archaeological surveys in the vicinity of Rosh Pinah show limited occupation of the dune sea margin, with most finds attributable to the late Holocene. A detailed survey of the 60km² area to be affected by the Skorpion Zinc mine and refinery (Kinahan 1997) revealed 41 archaeological sites, with more than half attributable to the late Holocene. These sites were strongly associated with isolated rocky outcrops among the dunes, and included surface scatters of stone artefact debris, stone windbreaks, and the remains of a hunting blind (Kinahan & Kinahan 2000). Limited surveys of potential landfill sites at Rosh Pinah (Kinahan 2001) indicated similar site distributions.

Among the archaeological sites documented in the course of these surveys, only one, a small cave, merited excavation. Skorpion Cave (27° 53.37'S 16° 38.74'E) lies just below the summit of a prominent feature known as Eccles Ridge, and faces the escarpment, some 5km to the northeast. Geologically, the site is unusual, having been formed by the erosion of a deep cavity in the limb of an antiform, so that the hillslope below the cave lies parallel rather than perpendicular to the dip of the strata. The rock strata comprise successive rhyolites and quartzites of the Gariep Complex, and it appears that a semi-vertical fault at the rear of the cave was responsible for their erosion by the flow of an artesian spring, now long extinct.

STRATIGRAPHY AND DATING

Excavation of Skorpion Cave was confined to a 3m² trench between the rear of the cave and the drip-line, and a 1m² test pit on the talus slope below the cave. Probing of the cave floor indicated that the trench covered the only part of the deposit suitable for excavation. The deposit in the trench comprised a well-stratified series of sandy and sandy ash layers with good organic preservation. The deposit had a maximum depth of 0.5m, and rested on weathered bedrock. Roofspalls and large rocks detached from the walls of the cave were found throughout the deposit. The talus slope below the cave was evidently part of the area of occupation, and the soil contained an unstratified admixture of stone artefact debris, pottery fragments and finely comminuted shell from land snails. Figure 1 shows the cave profile and stratigraphic sections, while Figure 2 shows the cave floor plan and talus slope features.

The base of the cave deposit (Unit 1) consisted of decomposed bedrock with loosely cemented sand, discoloured by yellowish groundwater precipitates. Above this was a continuous layer (Unit 2) of windblown sand with roof spalls. A radiocarbon sample from this unit yielded a date of 1340 ± 60 BP (Beta-160049) with a two sigma calendric calibration of AD 620 to 790 (Cal 1330 to 1160 years BP). The radiocarbon sample was associated with ceramics and antelope bone as well as other archaeological materials, as described below. Despite similarity in colour and texture, there was clear stratigraphic separation of this context and the overlying sediments (Unit 3). A compact layer (Unit 4) overlay Unit 3, mainly at the rear of the cave and at the drip-line.

Discrete concentrations of sandy ash (Unit 5), representing hearth accumulations, were found in hollowed areas of Unit 4. A radiocarbon sample from the upper surface of one hearth yielded a date of 180 ± 50 BP (Beta - 160048) with a two sigma calendric calibration of AD1640 to 1950 (Cal 310 to 0 years BP). This date is taken to represent the age of the loose and archaeologically poor surface material in Units 6 and 7. The stratigraphy and dating of the deposit indicates an undifferentiated occupation in the middle of the first millennium AD, and an historically recent occupation associated with the second radiocarbon date. The volume, depth and predominant colour of the seven units of stratigraphy recognised in the excavation are summarised in Table 1.

Table 5.1: *Comparison of stratigraphic units in excavation trench*

Unit	Volume (m³)	Max depth (m)	Colour (Munsell)
1	0.061	0.389	7.5 YR (5/4)
2	0.131	0.333	7.5 YR (4/3)
3	0.125	0.207	7.7 YR (4/3)
4	0.055	0.081	7.5 YR (4/4)
5	0.065	0.169	7.5 YR (8/2)
6	0.105	0.034	7.5 YR (4/3)
7	0.045	0.019	7.5 YR (4/3)

More detailed analysis was carried out on bulk soil samples from Units 1, 3, 4 and 6. Standard granulometric analyses, based on dry sieving with mesh sizes ranging from 25µm to 2800µm, showed a distinct bimodal particle size distribution for all four samples. The course fraction contained roof spall granules of 1 phi (2mm) diameter and greater, while the fine fraction comprised fine particles of 3 phi (125 μm) diameter and less, representing Aeolian deposition from the adjacent dunes. Moment statistics based on these analyses are presented in Table 2, together with soil nutrient analyses of the same samples.

Soil pH, nitrogen and phosphorus were determined by reflectometery, using proprietary Merck test strips. The soils were mildly alkaline, as is typical for the area. Nitrogen levels were highest in Unit 4, reflecting a high wood ash content in the occupation layers; and phosphorus levels were consistent with human occupation, although the somewhat higher phosphorus levels in Unit 7 probably reflect the use of the cave by antelope as a resting place, as indicated by the accumulation of dung pellets on the soil surface.

Table 5.2: *Analysis of bulk soil samples*

Unit	pH	NO$_2$ Mg/l	PO$_4$ Mg/l	Mean μm	Skewness	Kurtosis
1	9.2	2.4	65.0	95.42	1.22	1.45
3	9.6	3.0	66.0	84.10	1.86	2.79
4	9.3	4.0	69.0	83.51	2.12	4.97
6	9.5	3.5	76.0	91.15	1.28	0.68

ARTEFACT ASSEMBLAGES

A small sample of microlithic Later Stone Age artifacts was recovered from the deposit and from the talus slope below the cave. The artifacts were associated with material from three pottery vessels. Artefacts from shell and bone are described in the section dealing with organic remains.

Lithics

The stone tool assemblage was based on a combination of raw materials, including quartzite, probably from stream cobbles, hyrothermal vein quartz obtained from weathered exposures on the surrounding hillsides, as well as crystalline quartz and an array of cryptocrystalline silicate material such as chalcedony. These two latter raw materials have highly desirable flaking properties, and were brought to the site as small cobbles, possibly from well beyond the immediate vicinity of the site. A few pieces of haematite were also recovered from the deposit. The selection of lithic raw materials used at the site is presented in Table 3 according to reduction state and stratigraphic order.

Table 5. 3: *Analysis of lithic raw materials (abundance values for: a. cores; b. debitage; c. utilised pieces)*

Unit	Vein quartz a b c			Crystal quartz a b c			Quartzite a b c			Crypt. silicate a b c			Other
1	0	9	0	0	0	0	0	3	0	0	0	0	0
2	0	410	1	1	55	1	0	26	1	3	27	1	0
3	3	290	5	4	38	1	0	8	1	1	57	4	3*
4	0	26	0	0	2	0	0	0	0	0	1	0	0
5	0	53	0	0	5	0	0	1	0	0	6	2	0
6	0	156	0	1	13	1	0	5	0	0	13	1	1**
7	0	48	0	1	2	0	0	1	1	0	5	0	0
Talus	4	1	0	6	0	1	1	0	0	4	2	5	0

*   1 piece muscovite mica; 2 pieces specular haematite
**   1 piece haematite ochre

Hydrothermal vein quartz was the most abundant lithic raw material, although there were relatively few cores. This suggests that vein quartz was mainly used to produce informal pieces. Quartzite has similarly inferior flaking properties to vein quartz and its relative scarcity in the deposit probably reflects the greater availability of vein quartz in the near vicinity of the site. Crystal quartz and cryptocrystalline silicate were almost equally abundant. Cores and core fragments in crystal quartz were primarily used for bladelet production.

Typologically formal stone artifacts recovered from the deposits are listed in Table 4. All five scrapers were made from cryptocrystalline silicate, with en ecaille retouch on a curved section of the flake margin, using the side of the flake in four cases and the end of the flake in one case. The mean scraper length measured on the striking axis was 13.8 ± 2.8mm, and the breadth as measured perpendicular to the same axis was 14.8 ± 4.4mm (n. = 5). All of the scrapers showed clear indications of edge polish under 20 x magnification, but no traces of hafting mastic were observed. One other formal artefact in cryptocrystalline silicate was a borer measuring 13.5mm in length (snapped) and 4.4mm in breadth. The borer was made on a bladelet flake trimmed to a roughly parallel-sided shape. The only formal artefact in crystalline quartz was a segment made on a bladelet flake, measuring 13.2mm in length and 3.7mm in breadth. Finally, two ground stone artifacts were found on the surface of the cave deposit: a flat mortar stone and a pestle made from an unshaped quartzite river cobble.

Table 5.4: *Distribution of formal stone artifacts*

Unit	Scrapers	Segments	Borers
3	2	0	1
5	2	0	0
Talus	1	1	0

Ceramics

A total of 86 pottery sherds were recovered from the site, with 60% of these collected from the surface of the talus slope. A further 19% were found on the surface within the cave, or excavated from Unit 7. Sherds from Unit 6 made up another 8% of the total sample. The bulk of the ceramics from the site may therefore be attributed to the more recent occupation of the site, only 13% of the sample being firmly associated with the first occupation level. Three ceramic vessels could be identified from among the sherds found in the excavation and on the talus slope.

Vessel 1

The vessel is represented by a single rim sherd. A number of body sherds could be from the same vessel on the basis of fabric, the presence of soot encrustation (absent from the other two vessels) and stratigraphic position. Of the 16 body sherds assigned to this vessel eight were found within the cave in stratified context. The vessel rim is tapered and slightly bevelled. There is a shallow trimming groove on the outside and about 13mm below the rim; body thickness at the rim is 7.5mm, and below the rim groove 6.5mm.

The fabric of the vessel is remarkably fine and there is no trace of quartz temper. In section the sherds appear to have been fired in a reducing atmosphere, although the encrustation of soot indicates use as a cooking vessel, and this may have darkened the fabric. Vessel 1 is firmly associated with the earlier of the two radiocarbon dates reported above.

Vessel 2

The vessel is represented by three rim sherds, as well as a small neck sherd and three sherds belonging (but not conjoined) to a lug. The rim is slightly thickened and bevelled, but has no trimming groove. Body thickness at the rim is 7.0mm. From the fragments recovered, the lug was of the externally-applied and horizontally-pierced variety described by Rudner (1968: 619). These diagnostic features point to a small-necked pot, globular in shape, with lugs placed above the shoulder.

The fabric of the vessel is fine but it contains a small admixture of fine quartz. There are numerous small cavities in the fabric and it is possible that these contained organic matter that was destroyed in the process of firing. The rich reddish colour of the pottery is consistent with firing in an oxidizing atmosphere. Moreover, there is no trace of soot on either the inner or outer surfaces of the sherds, indicating that the vessel was used for storage rather than cooking. Sherds of this vessel, easily recognised by their colour, were found on the talus slope and on the surface within the cave. Of the 23 body sherds assigned to this vessel all but seven were found on the talus slope. Two sherds of Vessel 2 excavated within the cave were associated with the more recent of the two radiocarbon dates reported above.

Vessel 3

Diagnostic sherds from this vessel include three pieces of tapered rim, slightly thickened on the outside. The thickness of the rim and of the body below the rim is 5.5mm. A pronounced curve of the body below the rim suggests a low-necked pot, while the curve of the rim itself indicates a narrow mouth. The small size of the pot, its thin walls and lack of soot encrustation, together with a highly burnished outer surface, suggests that this was a storage vessel. All but four sherds assigned to this vessel were found on the talus slope.

Organic Remains

The deposit contained a fragmented but generally well-preserved assemblage of faunal remains, and a small quantity of identifiable plant material. The faunal assemblage comprised bones of various mammal and reptile species, as well as shell from ostrich eggs and land snails. The bone material belonged to the following taxa and skeletal elements, presented according to stratigraphic order:

Mammalia

Leporidae
Gen. et. sp. indet
Unit 2: left distal tibia and left distal ulna.
Unit 4: proximal radius.

Muridae
Gen. et sp. indet
Unit 2: assorted long bone fragments.
Unit 4: various mandible fragments without dentition.

Parotomys brantsii
Unit 4: left and right mandibles with dentition.
Unit 5: right mandible with dentition.
Unit 6: maxilla with dentition.

Canidae
Gen. et sp. indet
Unit 5: distal metatarsus

Procaviidae
Procavia capensis
Unit 5: left maxilla without dentition.

Bovidae
Size class 1 (cf. Brain 1974) *gen. et sp. indet.*

Unit 2: left coronoid and auricular; medial rib fragments; distal metatarsal fragment; phalange 1 (6 specimens); phalange 2 (4 specimens); phalange 3 (4 specimens).

Unit 4: phalange 3 (1 specimen).
Unit 5: right distal tibia fragment.

The rodent material from the deposit is almost certainly derived from disaggregated owl pellets. The identification of Brants' whistling rat *Parotomys barantsii* is based on the diagnostic laminae of the cheek teeth, as described by de Graaf (1981: 158). The presence of this species may reflect a slightly higher average rainfall than occurs today (cf. Smithers 1971), or seasonal range extensions from the desert margins. Seasonal abundance of food as a result of high winter rainfall might also explain the presence of hare and Rock dassie *Procavia capensis*.

Bovid material from the deposit is probably attributable to Steenbuck *Raphiceros campestris*, although the assemblage did not contain sufficient dignostic material to resolve this identification. Comparative measurements of the first and second phalange from four other species are presented in Table 4, undifferentiated as to manus and pes. Although these measurements do not match those of Walker (1985: 188), they appear to exclude the possibility of domestic sheep or goat in the deposit.

Table 5.5: *Comparison of bovid first and second phalange measurements*

Specimen	Phalange 1 Mean ± Std Dev. (n)	Phalange 2 Mean ± Std Dev. (n)
Skorpion Cave	28.8 ± 1.8 (6)	19.8 ± 1.5 (4)
Ovis aries	32.8 ± 0.4 (4)	19.6 ± 0.3 (4)
Capra hirca	34.9 ± 0.6 (2)	25.7 ± 2.2 (2)
Oreotragus oreotragus	33.4 ± 0.4 (8)	23.2 ± 0.2 (8)
Antidorcas marsupialis	35.4 ± 0.7 (6)	23.1 ± 0.1 (3)

Reptilia

Unidentified tortoise plastron fragments from Unit 4 exhibited slight traces of surface polish such as would be caused by use as a receptacle, implying that the tortoise could have been obtained elsewhere. Unidentified lizard mandibles found in Unit 6 are probably from disaggregated owl pellets.

Aves

Small quantities of ostrich eggshell were found throughout the deposit, with less than half showing discolouration due to charring. This would indicate that most of the eggshells were retained for use as vessels. An eggshell flask was reconstructed from fragments found among the rocks in the vicinity of the cave. Fragments of broken shells were used to make beads, and the distribution and size range of beads recovered from the excavation is presented in Table 5.5. The bead measurements show no significant size variation across the excavated sequence.

Table 5.6: *Distribution of ostrich eggshell fragments and beads*

Unit	Fragments g Fresh (% burnt)	Beads Ømm Mean ± Std Dev. (n)
1	4.2 (9.52)	(0)
2	1118.6 (15.94)	5.3 ± 0.1 (2)
3	74.4 (4.97)	6.6 ± 2.2 (11)
4	52.7 (4.93)	7.9 ± 1.6 (8)
5	45.6 (32.0)	8.9 ± 0.5 (6)
6	168.8 (8.12)	7.6 ± 0.9 (10)
7	223.0 (0.9)	8.6 ± 0.9 (2)

Mollusca

Significant concentrations of shell from land snails Trigonephrus cf. haughtoni were found in the cave deposit. A total of 278 entire shells was recovered, as well as an equally large number of aperture fragments from broken specimens. More than 50% of the shells were found in Unit 3, with 31% from Unit 2 and 17% from Unit 6. Further concentrations of shells were found on the talus slope and a test pit over 1m² yielded a total of 281 specimens. In size, the shells showed little variation, those from the cave deposit having a mean length of 15.2 ± 1.6mm (n. = 278), compared with 16.4 ± 1.5mm (n. -= 281) for those from the talus slope test pit.

A large proportion of the shells showed evidence of charring. This, and the higher concentration of shells at the site compared with the surrounding dune fields, suggests that the snails were gathered as food. The dense accumulations of shell suggests that snails were processed on the talus slope as well as in the cave itself. The dispersion of pottery sherds on the talus slope does not closely coincide with the positioning of the shell accumulations, as it might be if the pottery was used to cook snails. Instead, the snails appear to have been cooked in their shells, while at least two of the three pottery vessels were used for storage rather than food preparation.

One specimen of a cowrie *Cypraea spp.*, possibly originating from the Indian Ocean coast, was found on the talus slope below the cave. The dorsal surface of the cowrie has been removed by grinding, to allow the shell to be threaded. A fragment of a marine limpet *Patella spp,* indicating contact with the Atlantic coast, was recovered from Unit 4.

Plant Remains

The only identifiable plant remains recovered from the deposit were seed cases. Of these more than 90% (n. = 153) were !nara melon Acathsicyos horrida, the remainder being tsamma melon (citrillus lanatus (n = 11), and one suspected castor oil bean Ricinus communis. Seed cases of !nara were most abundant in Units 4, 5 and 6. One living specimen of the !nara plant has been recorded in the vicinity of the Skorpion Zinc mine site (B. Curtis, *pers. comm.*).

DISCUSSION

The excavation of Skorpion Cave provides new evidence of hunter-gatherer settlements and subsistence on the edge of the southern Namib Desert during the first two millennia AD. The general picture that emerges from the excavation is of highly opportunistic subsistence activity in response to winter rainfall events. Although hunter-gatherers would have pursued migratory antelope and other large species attracted to the area after the rains, the evidence from the cave shows that smaller animals provided the mainstay of the diet. This, in turn, suggests that hunter-gatherer occupation of the cave was on too small a scale to permit cooperative hunting of large game species.

The lack of water in the vicinity of the site would have been an important limiting factor and it is quite probable that occupation was confined to short stops in the course of hunting and food-gathering expeditions. Smaller antelope, such as the Steenbok *Raphiceros campestris*, suspected as one of the species among the faunal remains, would not require cooperative hunting, and neither would hare nor Rock dassie *Procavia capensis*. Indeed, the presence of a single dassie maxilla raises the possibility that the animal was brought to the site from the escarpment, perhaps in the form of provisions. The same would apply to the presence of melon seeds, particularly those of the !nara Acanthsiyos horrida. These require time-consuming preparation, and due to the weight and bulk of the melons, as well as the need for wood fuel to cook them, such activity would take place where the melons grew and not at the cave site.

Of particular interest among the food remains are the land snails Trigonephrus cf. haughtoni. The specimens from Skorpion Cave were somewhat smaller than those measured by Dallas and Curtis (1991: 108) in which the mean length of the shells was 34.4 ± 2.0mm (n. = 100). The species prefers thinly vegetated dunes and is not generally found on high rocky hillslopes. Dallas and Curtis (1991: 112) recorded patch densities of snails with a mean of 4.3 ± 3.3 specimens/m² (n.=25). Although highly noticeable, these patches have a far lower density than those recorded at Skorpion Cave. Moreover, clear evidence of charring shows that the snails were cooked, probably in their shells. Dallas and Curtis (1991) state that Trigonephrus is most active in winter, when it feeds from new plant growth, and this is when it would have been most easily gathered by people.

The fact that land snails have not been recorded elsewhere in Namibia as a significant food resource on an archaeological site underlines the opportunistic and rather marginal nature of hunter-gatherer subsistence on the edge of the dune sea. Indeed, if the evidence from Skorpion Cave reflects the re-occupation of the area following the late Holocene hiatus, conditions must have remained highly variable at that time. It is also possible that intermittent occupation of the area continued during the period of the supposed hiatus, in response to short pulses of climatic amelioration. More systematic survey of the southern Namib Desert margin, focusing on small sites located in areas of high potential response to rainfall, would provide a finer resolution of the sequence and human adaptation to this environment.

REFERENCES

Brain, C.K. (1974)
"Some Suggested Procedures in the Analysis of Bone Accumulations From Southern African Quaternary Sites." *Annals of the Transvaal Museum* 29 (1): 1-8

Dallas, H.F. and Curtis, B.A. (1991)
"Shell Distribution of the Terrestrial Snail, *Trigonephrus Sp*. (Mollusca: Dorcasiidae) in The Southern Namib Dunes." *Cimbebasia* 13: 105-115.

De Graaf, G. (1981)
The rodents of southern Africa. Durban, Butterworth, pp 267.

Kinahan, J. (1997)
Skorpion Zinc Environmental Impact Study: Archaeological Survey. Quaternary Research Services (Namibia) Report 12. Commissioned by WSP Walmsley Environmental Consultants (Pty) Ltd., Johannesburg, pp 26.

Kinahan, J. (2001)
Archaeological assessment of proposed landfill sites at Rosh Pinah. Quaternary Research Services (Namibia) Report 26. Commissioned by WSP Walmsley (Pty) Ltd., Johannesburg, pp 15.

Kinahan, J. and Kinahan, J. (2000)
Archaeological Mitigation of the Skorpion Zinc Project. Quaternary Researhc Services (Namibia) Report 20. Commissioned by Bateman Engineering Ltd. And Reunion Mining (Namibia) (Pty) Ltd. Pp 14.

Rudner, J. (1968)
Strandloper pottery from South and South West Africa. Annals of the South African Museum 49 (2): 441-663,

Sievers, K. (1984)
Test excavations at Rosh Pinah Shelter, southern Namibia. In Kinahan, J. ed. Recent archaeological research between the Orange and Kavango Rivers in southwestern Africa. State Museum of Namibia, Cimbebasia Ser. B (4) 3: 29-40.

Smithers, R. (1971)
The mammals of Botswana. Memoir, National Museum of Rhodesia 4: 1-340.

Vogel, J.C. and Visser, E. (1981)
Pretoria radiocarbon dates II. Radiocarbon 23: 43-80.

Walker, R. (1985)
A guide to post-cranial bones of East African mammals. Norwich, Hylochoerus, pp 285.

Wendt, W.E. (1972)
Preliminary report on a research programme in South West Africa. Cimbebasia B 2 (1): 1-61.

6

La Poterie Locale des Hautes Terres Centrales de I'Imerina (Madagascar): Identification de Groupes ou Mobilier Artistique

Darsot Rasolofomampianina Léon

Abstract This chapter deals with some aspects of local pottery from the central highlands of Imerina (Madagascar). Local pottery translates technical skills as well as artistic creativity of ancient population. However, ceramic is witnessing not only art, but is a fundamental element in social and economical organisation in ancient Imerina.

Ceramic, with its various decorations, went through different historical times and gives precious information on forgotten ways of life that archaeology has unearthed. Common or local pottery, witnesses different groups of population who lived in ancient Imerina. Motifs of decoration have marked different periods, either for aesthetic or for common production; their diversification and diffusion suggests circulation of population as well as of goods during cultural phases when self-sufficiency was always thought to be fundamental.

INTRODUCTION

Ce travail reprend en partie avec des modifications du texte original, un mémoire d'étude pour l'obtention d'une maîtrise en archéologie intitulée: Les décors céramique sur la poterie locale de l'Imerina ancien : *Les collections de l'Institut de Civilisations - Musée d'Art et d'Archéologie* soutenue en mai 2001 à l'Université d'Antananarivo, Département de Civilisations.

La céramique ou la poterie a toujours tenu un rôle capital dans tous les travaux archéologiques. En plus de ce problème posé par la quantité de poteries non traitées et étudiées, il était donc préférable de se limiter aux collections déjà entreposées dans les réserves, en particulier celle de l'Institut de Civilisations-

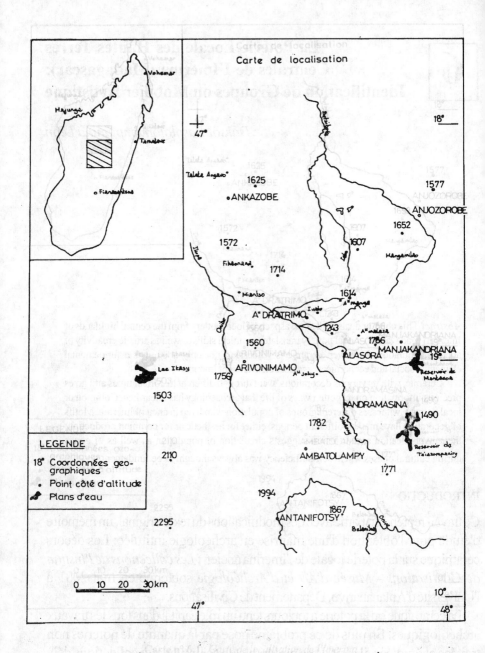

Carte n° 6.1 : *Carte de localisation de l'Imerina*

Musée d'Art et d'Archéologie (IC/MAA), de les analyser et de poursuivre éventuellement des fouilles.

Cette orientation des travaux archéologiques s'explique par le nombre élevé d'objets en terre cuite récoltés ou exhumés lors des campagnes de fouilles archéologiques ou durant les reconnaissances. Un classement des collections figure parmi les travaux de l'IC/MAA ainsi que celui des sites ayant fait l'objet de fouille ou de reconnaissance. Une mise à jour des données était donc nécessaire dans le domaine des travaux archéologiques. L'archéologie fut souvent un parent pauvre des études universitaires à Madagascar car ses objectifs et sa finalité étaient toujours mal compris dans un pays où la priorité est d'ordre économique et social.

A partir des années soixante-dix, l'archéologie a fait des progrès remarquables. De nouvelles méthodes de prospection furent mises en pratique comme les survey, c'est-à-dire une approche plus intensive des régions et des sites où chaque élément est répertorié tant en surface qu'en profondeur. En effet, les traces des anciennes occupations humaines peuvent se retrouver en profondeur et être mises au jour par les fouilles et les sondages, mais d'autres éléments pouvant permettre de retracer cette occupation et le système d'organisation socio-spatiale peuvent être appréhendés en surface. Les pierres levées, marques de séparation d'espace, de territoire ou faisant l'objet de culte, apportent des informations pour la reconstitution du passé d'une région; les tombeaux, leurs formes, leur évolution architecturale, leur localisation dans l'espace sont autant d'éléments susceptibles de fournir des explications.

Les nouvelles techniques de datation ont d'autre part grandement contribué à cet essor de l'archéologie malgache. Pourtant, cette masse énorme d'informations qu'elle représente pouvait aussi être une difficulté pour son étude.

Nous avons choisi l'Imerina même si cette région a déjà fait l'objet de nombreux travaux[1] basés sur la céramique. Les études traitant de la poterie sont assez notables, que ce soit sous forme de communications, de rapports de fouille ou de publications scientifiques. Déjà en 1898, le Capitaine Ferry a fait une publication,[2] sur la céramique de la région d'Antananarivo. Les travaux de Vérin (1968-1970), de Mantaux (1969) et de Mille (1969-1970) ont beaucoup apporté à la connaissance des anciens sites fortifiés de l'Imerina, à l'interprétation des habitats anciens, des vestiges matériels et culturels qui y ont été récoltés. Les récents travaux de Rasamuel[3] sur Fanongoavana et de Wright[4] sur les poteries de l'Imerina ancien ont réaffirmé les connaissances pour l'étude de la poterie car la technique de fabrication est mieux appréhendée ainsi que la possibilité d'élaborer une typologie des formes de la poterie locale et d'établir un début de chronologie.

IMPORTANCE DE L'ETUDE

La poterie est par définition la combinaison d'une matière première: l'argile, de forme et de décoration. Ces éléments imprégnés sur la poterie sont le reflet d'une certaine idée, d'une habitude d'un groupe pendant une période donnée, d'une zone géographique. L'étude des éléments typologiques constitue une part importante dans l'interprétation de la céramique. Une poterie peut être copiée, à l'instar de tout autre objet en circulation dans une société. Aussi des parentés formelles et techniques existent-elles parmi les vestiges de poterie découverts, par exemple au niveau du façonnage ou des dessins décoratifs. Cependant, il faut se garder de faire des rapprochements hâtifs car deux poteries, ayant des ressemblances formelles peuvent ne pas appartenir à une même période.[5] Ces parentés techniques et formelles entre les tessons de poterie découverts peuvent se retrouver mais chaque tesson est unique dans son genre car c'est un produit artisanal et non industriel durant l'époque ancienne. Les techniques de fabrication se déplacent probablement.[6] Mais les artisans s'attachent très longtemps à une technique qui a fait ses preuves. Plusieurs générations peuvent donc se succéder sans qu'il y ait modification notable de l'objet. A cette hypothèse vient s'ajouter l'importance des sites dans leur environnement politique et économique ou l'influence d'un groupe et par conséquent l'influence d'un style tend à se vulgariser tant à l'intérieur qu'à l'extérieur de son aire de fabrication. Une mode artistique commencera à prendre forme dans le cas où l'on essayera d'imiter la forme la plus en vogue. La propagation d'un style ira de pair avec le rayonnement socio-économique d'une entité sociale influente. Une population a tendance à vouloir copier un fait ou un élément de société qui a marqué son époque et à cela s'ajoutent l'importance et le rayonnement socio-économique des sites dans l'espace géographique. Replacer la poterie et les décors qui l'accompagnent dans leur cadre historique est donc nécessaire, car cette démarche peut apporter des éclaircissements sur le passé d'une population, voire le peuplement d'une région. L'élaboration d'une typologie des décors permettra par ailleurs de mettre en évidence les mutations ou la pérennité de ces témoins culturels ou leur disparition.

PROBLEMATIQUE

La dynamique de la poterie traditionnelle ne peut se comprendre qu'en relation avec l'importance régionale des sites et des conditions générales du pays. Les populations s'approprient cette expansion des techniques et des décorations par assimilation ou par contact avec des milieux différents. Une assimilation à la fois des techniques et des oeuvres d'art conduit à la maintenance d'un style dans la région ou dans les zones avoisinantes.

Les variétés dans les styles et dessins sur la céramique locale sont-elles caractéristiques d'une période ou d'une phase de peuplement bien définie et devenues la propriété de la population ou bien sont-elles le résultat d'une migration de styles ? Les motifs sont-ils apparentés à une fonction ou comme mobilier de décoration ou l'appartenance à un groupe ?

LA CIRCULATION DES POTERIES

Des Origines Encore Mal Connues

Pour les Hautes Terres Centrales, en particulier l'Imerina, les travaux et études faites par Wright (1979) sur la poterie locale sont déterminantes et d'une grande utilité. Il a pu établir une chronologie relative des sites en relation avec des phases culturelles. Elle reflète les séquences typologiques, les relations culturelles dans le temps à partir des similitudes, des différences entre les types, les styles ou les attributs qui sont relativement proches dans le temps et dans l'espace:

- La phase Fiekena pour les plus anciennes et antérieures au XVIème siècle;
- La phase Ankatso pour la période du XVIème siècle;
- La phase Angavobe pour la période fin XVIème - première moitié du XVIIème siècle;
- La phase Ambohidray allant de la fin du XVIIème au début du XVIIIème siècle;
- La phase Kaloy vers la deuxième moitié du XVIIIème à la première moitié du XIXème siècle;
- La phase Fiadanana à partir du milieu du XIXème siècle.

La poterie locale a pu être reconstituée à partir des vestiges qui ont été assemblés ou à partir des objets de fouille intacts. Des formes originales apparaissent comme les assiettes à pieds, les loviamanga, qui sont des assiettes caractéristiques de la phase Ankatso (XVIème siècle). Elles sont enduites d'un graphite noir et brillant.

Les poteries finement décorées se retrouvent dans les sites anciennement occupés. Les décors sont en grande majorité faites d'impressions triangulaires. Les datations sur le site d'Analamanitra attestent que les loviamanga décorés sont du XIVème siècle.

Elles peuvent être fabriquées dans des centres de production et échangées à plus ou moins grande distance, comme produits de vente ou de troc. On a toujours pensé que la poterie, de diffusion restreinte et d'usage local, ne se déplaçait pas. Cette hypothèse était présente car les informations recueillies jusqu'à présent se rapportant aux déplacements des populations étaient encore réduites. Le niveau technique permettant une grande production était encore aléatoire durant ces périodes, malgré la bonne qualité des produits. Certes, les études sur la circulation des poteries sont encore insuffisantes voire inexistantes, mais il y avait nécessairement un mouvement de la poterie même si l'origine des " importations " est très proche, car malgré l'abondance des poteries et des tessons sur les sites, rares sont ceux sur lesquels on a trouvé des fours à potier ou des lieux d'extraction de l'argile comme à Fanongoavana[7] ou dans la région du Manandriana sur le site de Vohimalaza.[8] En outre, la présence des restes de boules d'argile cuite découvertes sur des habitats anciens attestent cette présence de fabrication.[9]

Des traces d'ateliers spécialisés n'ont pas encore été mis au jour, et l'on suppose que les ateliers à caractère familial ne produisaient que des produits nécessaires aux besoins quotidiens de la population de la région. De par sa fonction de contenant, la production de poterie ne devait pas donc faire, dans cette hypothèse, l'objet d'un commerce fructueux, ou au plus on pourrait penser à une économie de troc sur un plan local.

Migrations des Poteries et Populations

Le déplacement des poteries est toujours en relation avec les mouvements de personnes. La précarité des zones de peuplements anciens est un des facteurs de migration des poteries. Lorsque la zone d'implantation ne peut plus satisfaire aux besoins de cette population, celle-ci se déplace en emportant avec elles ses richesses, ses connaissances et ses habitudes. La non satisfaction peut être occasionnée par des habitudes communautaires qui font diminuer les ressources locales en nourriture. La pratique de brûlis fait disparaître et diminuer progressivement l'espace nourricier de la population : les ressources de la chasse et de la cueillette se font rares et les champs se stérilisent.

La recherche de nouveaux espaces est donc une nécessité pour les anciennes populations. Les troubles entre communautés pour l'acquisition de nouveaux terrains d'occupation figurent aussi dans ces facteurs de déplacement de personnes. L'environnement et l'économie limitent la taille et la permanence du peuplement parce que la capacité de rassembler et de stocker la nourriture est aussi importante que la technique nécessaire pour transporter et la transformer en forme comestible.

La production de poterie est intégrée dans un processus économique. En effet, elle répond à une satisfaction de besoins d'une population donnée. C'est dans ce sens que les centres qui regroupent une population assez importante peuvent être des foyers de production ou d'échanges. La division de la société en différentes catégories intervient aussi dans la multiplication des formes et des décorations appliquées sur les poteries.

La fonction de la poterie et sa diffusion interviennent dans le processus socio-économique de la population. La poterie locale a trois fonctions bien définies : le stockage de produits (liquide ou solide), la transformation et en dernier lieu le transport.

Le stockage surtout en ce qui concerne les poteries des collections du Musée d'Art et d'Archéologie, touche plus particulièrement l'entreposage des eaux dans la maison avec les grandes jarres (*sinibe*).[10] La transformation se rapporte au mode d'utilisation des ustensiles en terre cuite pour la cuisson des aliments avec les marmites (*vilany*). Le transport est celui de l'approvisionnement en eau avec les cruches (*siny*). Ces rôles sont restreints à l'espace familial mais les ustensiles se déplaceront avec le groupe migrant vers une autre zone plus favorable à une nouvelle implantation permanente ou non.

Les similarités entre les styles ou décorations reflètent l'expression des relations entre différents groupes sociaux ou communautés. Lorsqu'une nouvelle forme et des décorations neuves étaient créées, il était facile de les imiter. Si on considère la majorité des poteries et des décorations, il ressort que les matériaux utilisés sont simples, matériaux en végétale comme des tiges de roseaux ou des petites lames de fer. Cette simplicité facilite la diffusion des décors par imitation car les outils sont courants. Cependant, en plus de cette production de caractère familial ou rural très disséminé, des centres plus importants se sont imposés à qui l'on doit cette homogénéité des productions à un niveau local ou régional.

Les modes d'utilisation des ustensiles en terre cuite peuvent déterminer les genres de décors. Les récipients employés pour la cuisson auront des formes et des décors différents de la vaisselle par exemple. Cette dernière a une apparence plus soignée car elle est destinée à servir et pour les repas. Sa forme, plus ouverte, se prête mieux à des décorations sur sa surface. Les faces intérieure et extérieure seront mieux élaborées. Les zones de décoration sont plus faciles à travailler par rapport aux récipients à parois arrondies comme les jarres. Ces zones seront plus faciles à diviser et à partager pour les motifs. La combinaison d'éléments est de fait facile à réaliser. Il est fréquent de voir des assiettes, des bols ou des écuelles avec des lèvres plus larges pour recevoir des motifs. Les jarres sont destinées au transport, donc elles ont besoin d'une surface non lisse et assez rugueuse. La décoration est faible, voire inexistante sur les parois. Elle est limitée aux traces de peignage qui confirme que cette caractéristique répond plus à des besoins pratiques, la maniabilité, qu'à l'esthétique. Il en sera de même pour un récipient avec un col haut. Il portera peu de décor sur sa partie haute même si la surface est nettement grande. Mais le décor se retrouvera au niveau de l'épaule car la surface est plus ou moins aplatie et le regard se porte automatiquement sur cette partie du récipient. Il en sera aussi pour la panse jusqu'au niveau de l'arrondi de la base. Cependant on ne retrouve plus la symétrie au niveau de la répétition des motifs comme dans le cas des poteries de la phase Fiekena, antérieure au XVème siècle.

Il est cependant difficile de reconnaître l'origine d'une forme ou même d'un décor car chacun apportera sa petite touche personnelle face à la concurrence due à l'imitation. L'origine d'un style de décoration ou d'une forme de poterie est l'œuvre d'un groupe. Elle s'est établie à partir d'étapes successives, d'inventions et d'améliorations progressives. Le style s'est stabilisé par la suite si le support, la poterie, est adaptée aux usages requis ou souhaités par la population. Il ne faut pas oublier que la poterie doit être en premier lieu un objet utile, durable et enfin beau. Sa diffusion n'est donc que le résultat des satisfactions qu'elle accorde.

Dans leur ouvrage sur la poterie, M.H et J. Santrot (1979) soulignent à juste titre que: "*les techniques de fabrication et de décoration reflètent l'acquis technologique d'une population et marquent pour une part, son évolution culturelle.*"

Le style décoratif est sans cesse en évolution. Il peut être soumis à des variations et des modifications dues à la plus ou moins grande aptitude des individus à le reproduire, mais nous pensons que ce dynamisme est dû au sens de l'innovation de l'artisan.

L'origine d'un style de décoration ou d'une forme de poterie est l'œuvre d'une création d'un groupe. Mais dans la plupart des cas, si le dessin des motifs reste le même, les techniques inhérentes à chaque matière, imposent des solutions propres et aboutissent à une variété des répertoires de décors. Toutefois le potier suit l'évolution des besoins et du goût de la société.

Nous avons mentionné que lorsqu'un style de décoration est créé, il était facile à chacun de l'imiter et sa pérennité s'explique par la qualité technique et par la meilleure réponse aux goûts de l'époque. La disparition ou l'expansion d'une forme et/ou d'un décor est le reflet des besoins et des goûts de la population. La céramique est ainsi indissociable de la vie culturelle des groupes de populations et d'une certaine manière, inséparable de la vie économique dans le cadre d'échange de production même local ou régional.

LA POTERIE LOCALE : UNE REFERENCE CHRONOLOGIQUE

Les données en notre possession ne nous permettent pas jusqu'ici d'avancer qu'il existait une concurrence, au sens économique du terme, entre différentes localités ou petits ateliers de production pouvant aboutir à la disparition d'un style et d'une forme de poterie. Il est probable qu'il existait des petits ateliers ruraux localisés ou des ateliers familiaux avec une production très diversifiée de formes mais contenant à quelques détails près les mêmes esquisses de décoration, car l'imitation était facile mais non la standardisation en grand nombre qui nécessitait la création d'ateliers plus grands et plus élaborés.

Fixation de Groupes

La céramique correspond à des sociétés sédentaires. C'est une série d'habitudes qui sont introduites, elle est profondément liée à l'organisation des sociétés pendant des siècles d'histoire. Elle est indicatrice sur la manière et les habitudes quotidiennes. Elles nous renseignent sur la façon des populations pour conserver, cuire, ou boire.... La céramique vulgaire ne voyage pas beaucoup parce qu'elle est lourde. C'est la fixation au sol. Nous avons alors la sédentarisation de l'homme à travers la céramique. De plus, un des grands inconvénients des pots en terre cuite est leur fragilité. Ce sont donc des ustensiles destinés à être placés dans un endroit sûr ou à manier délicatement pour éviter les cassures.

Bien de poteries ont eu une diffusion locale dont l'aire serait à peu près la même que l'ancien territoire du site. Elle pourrait correspondre à l'espace d'habitat et de travail du groupe. Cette distance correspond généralement à la zone d'influence d'un groupe ou d'un site dominant.

Cependant, cette circulation est sujette à des remarques et des critiques, mais faute d'une véritable étude archéométrique des poteries, nous nous devons d'être prudents dans notre démarche car il ne saurait être question de localiser avec précision les aires de fabrication. Les traditions orales ont complété cette lacune ainsi que la découverte de tessons pouvant servir de référence chronologique comme la poterie importée et ont permis de dégager des phases culturelles chronologiques, même si celles-ci sont encore relatives.

Cette continuité de la poterie locale en Imerina s'explique aussi par le fait que la qualité de la production et la présentation des poteries étaient rapidement acquises par la force de la tradition et transmises de génération en génération. En considérant les différentes décorations de la poterie locale de l'Imerina, on constate que les récipients en terre cuite les plus décorés sont des poteries qui remontent au Xème - XIVème siècles.

Les décors s'estompent peu à peu à mesure que l'on parcourt les périodes historiques récentes. Ainsi sur les poteries de la phase Fiekena, antérieure au XVème siècle, on a une impression de surabondance de décors faits de lignes géométriques incisées où se superposent de petites figures triangulaires, alors que pour la phase Fiadanana du milieu du XIXème siècle, les décorations deviennent plus rares, voire inexistantes. Le style de décoration est sans cesse en évolution. Elle peut être soumise à des variations et des modifications dues à la plus ou moins grande aptitude des individus à les reproduire, mais nous pensons surtout que ce dynamisme est dû à leur sens de l'innovation.

LE ROLE DES CAPITALES REGIONALES

Définition

Nous entendons par capitale régionale, un ancien site d'habitat qui avait un rayonnement socio-économique dans une région. Ce sont les anciens sites marqués par la personnalité d'un souverain important ou d'un groupe, surtout à partir de l'époque de la formation du royaume merina. Mais il ne faut pas oublier que des localités, avec des " souverains ", avaient déjà une notoriété réelle sur leurs populations et leur espace environnant bien avant cette époque comme les sites d'Ampandrana avec Rafandrana ou Fanongoavana avec Andrianamponga. Ces sites sont tous antérieurs à la période historique des royaumes merina.

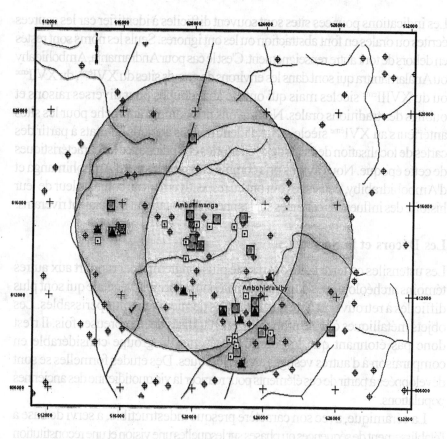

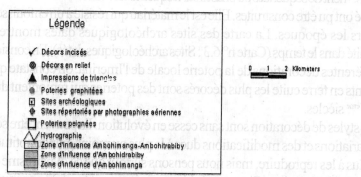

Carte n° 6.2 : *Zone d'influence d'Ambohimanga et Ambohidrabiby*

Les indications pour ces sites sont souvent difficiles à identifier car les sources écrites ou orales en font abstraction ou les ont ignorés. Seuls les noms sont restés en dehors de tout autre renseignement. C'est le cas pour Andramanja, Ambohidahy ou Analamanitra qui sont dans les environs de grands sites du XVIème, du XVIIème ou du XVIIIème siècles mais qui ont été abandonnés pour diverses raisons et oubliés des traditions orales. Nous avons pris comme approche pour les sites antérieurs au XVIème siècle, celle d'identifier ces anciens habitats à partir des cartes de localisation des sites déjà répertoriés et étudiés avec les caractéristiques de cette époque. Nous avions pris comme exemple les cas d'Ambohimanga et d'Ambohidrabiby, deux sites qui ont eu respectivement au cours de leur de leur histoire des influences certaines sur les anciens habitats qui leur étaient riverains.

Les Décors et la Société

Les ustensiles en terre cuite ont résisté plus longtemps par rapport aux autres témoins archéologiques comme les matériaux d'origine végétale qui sont plus difficiles à retrouver et à reconstituer. Ces derniers sont plus périssables. Les objets métalliques ont été probablement réutilisés de nombreuses fois. Il n'est donc pas étonnant que la poterie représente un groupe considérable en comparaison à d'autres vestiges archéologiques. Des études formelles se sont développées à partir de ces éléments pour retracer la vie quotidienne des anciennes populations.

La céramique, avec son caractère presque indestructible, a servi de base à l'établissement de séquences ou phases sur lesquelles une vision et une reconstitution du passé ont pu être construites. Elle est le matériau qui résiste à un enfouissement à travers les époques. La carte des sites archéologiques datés montre cette continuité dans le temps (Carte n° 6.3 : Sites archéologiques datés). En considérant les différentes décorations de la poterie locale de l'Imerina, on constate que les récipients en terre cuite les plus décorés sont des poteries qui remontent du Xème au XIVème siècles.

Les styles de décoration sont sans cesse en évolution. Ils peuvent être soumis à des variations et des modifications dues à la plus ou moins grande aptitude des individus à les reproduire, mais nous pensons surtout que ce dynamisme est dû au sens de l'innovation. C'est une évidence qui se maintient de nos jours que l'artiste tend à " une pureté des lignes " en abandonnant des détails qui ont été fixés auparavant pour servir de modèle.

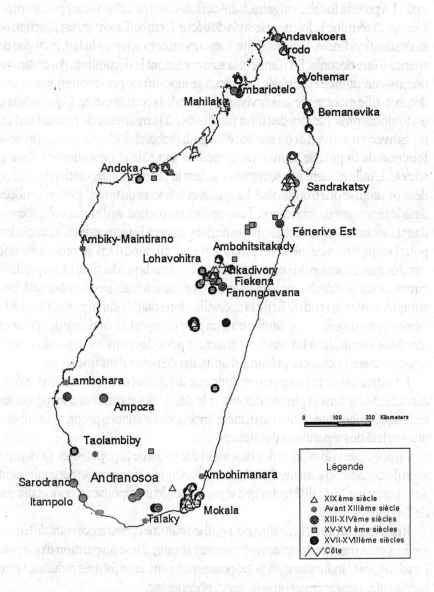

Sites archéologiques datés

Andavakoera
Irodo
Vohemar
Ambariotelo
Mahilaka
Bemanevika

Andoka
Sandrakatsy

Fénerive Est
Ambiky-Maintirano
Ambohitsitakady
Lohavohitra
Ankadivory
Fiekena
Fanongoavana

Lambohara
Ampoza

0   100   200 Kilometers

Taolambiby

Ambohimanara
Sarodrano
Andranosoa
Itampolo
Mokala
Talaky

Légende

△ XIXème siècle
● Avant XIIIème siècle
◉ XIII-XIVème siècles
■ XV-XVIème siècles
▲ XVII-XVIIIème siècles
∧ Côte

Carte n° 6.3 : *Sites archéologiques datés*

Rasamuel (1984) indique l'existence de deux genres de poteries sur les Hautes Terres centrales de l'Imerina : une poterie commune, vulgaire, et une poterie de luxe. La poterie locale, vulgaire, a été définie comme celle n'étant pas décorée. L'usage détermine la forme et le style de décor. L'embellissement est fonction de sa destination finale. Une marmite, toujours en contact avec le feu, aura peu de chance d'être décorée. La fumée et la suie cacheront la décoration. Au contraire, une assiette, utilisée et destinée à servir un groupe ou une petite communauté sera décorée. Elle montrera le savoir vivre et le goût de la communauté. Cette habitude est toujours présente lors des fêtes familiales où la maîtresse de maison sert les repas avec un couvert et un service d'un goût recherché. Ces habitudes, avec la fonction de la poterie, donne un aperçu de son rôle et de sa qualité dans la société. L'utile et l'agréable se retrouvent dans la poterie. La décoration traduit un désir ou une marque d'originalité. La qualité et la finesse du travail sont préconisées dans le processus de fabrication. Les poteries, commune ou de luxe, cohabiteront dans la société. Seulement, le niveau de richesse sera le facteur de différenciation pour l'acquisition de tel ou tel produit. Il y aurait donc dans ce processus une certaine spécialisation du potier ou de la potière dans la production. Deux produits circulent sur le marché, non qu'ils se concurrencent mais se complètent. Cette complémentarité rend difficile la spécialisation spatiale car la poterie peut être fabriquée au niveau d'une famille ou d'un petit groupe. L'abondance des poteries récoltées sur un site à travers les différentes périodes peuvent cependant nous renseigner sur l'existence présumé d'un atelier de potier dans une région.

La diffusion de la poterie n'est donc que le résultat des satisfactions qu'elle accorde. Mais dans la plupart des cas, si le dessin des motifs reste le même, les techniques inhérentes à chaque matière impose des solutions propres et aboutit à une variété des répertoires des décors.

Le potier suit l'évolution des besoins et des goûts de la population. Lorsqu'un style de décoration était né, il était facile à chacun de l'imiter et sa pérennité peut s'expliquer par la qualité technique et par la meilleure réponse au goût et usages de l'époque.

Il nous est encore difficile d'avancer qu'il existait une concurrence entre différents ateliers ou zones productrices qui pourrait aboutir à une disparition d'un style. Les données et indications en notre possession sont, en effet, très réduites, voire inexistantes pour affirmer ou infirmer ce phénomène.

Nous savons certes, d'une manière encore confuse, que les changements d'habitudes sociales de la population et des techniques de fabrication ont pu provoquer l'expansion ou la disparition progressive de certaines productions.

Le recul des habitudes de prendre des repas en commun, hormis durant les grandes fêtes traditionnelles, a développé une production plus grande des assiettes individuelles. Il est le reflet de la disparition de la vie communautaire au profit de la vie privée. La variété des modes alimentaires aussi a étendu le champ de la fabrication des marmites. Le développement des cultures et de l'élevage a donné naissance à une diversité des menus et à une spécialisation des ustensiles à employer. La découverte de nouveaux ustensiles plus durables et de bonne apparence peut éradiquer petit à petit la production des poteries traditionnelles. Les céramiques importées, chinoise, bleu-blanc du XIVème siècle ou européenne du XVIème siècle, auraient influencé fortement les fabricants locaux. Cette poterie en porcelaine ne se prêtait pas aux décorations traditionnelles des époques antérieures comme les incisions. Elle était faite de couleur appliquée. A partir de cette période, une attirance pour les poteries à surface lisse, graphitée se vulgarisent aux niveaux de la production.

La céramique devient un indice social important en fonction de la qualité et de la quantité de tessons découverts et des formes. C'est un indice social historique. Il est probable qu'il existait des petits ateliers ruraux ou familiaux avec une production très diversifiée de formes mais contenant à quelques détails près les mêmes formes de décoration, car l'imitation était facile. Ces caractères des ateliers de poterie signifiaient que seul le nécessaire était produit et ne faisait pas l'objet d'un commerce, au sens actuel du terme, mais d'un troc sur un plan local ou régional.

Il y eut donc nécessairement déplacement de poteries même si l'origine de ces migrations est très proche. Bon nombre de poteries ont une diffusion locale dont l'aire de propagation serait à peu près la même que l'espace social du site. L'aire d'expansion pourrait correspondre au territoire occupé par le groupe (Carte n° 6.4 : Répartition des poteries décorées).

La variété des formes, et implicitement les décors, sera un indice social extrêmement important pour l'archéologue et l'historien. C'est une indication sociale historique. On peut rencontrer des céramiques qui ne serviront à rien, sur le plan utilitaire, sinon pour la beauté de la demeure, et seront par définition des poteries fines ou céramique de décor.[13] La céramique de luxe est une céramique qui sert à embellir comme la vaisselle, les coupes…

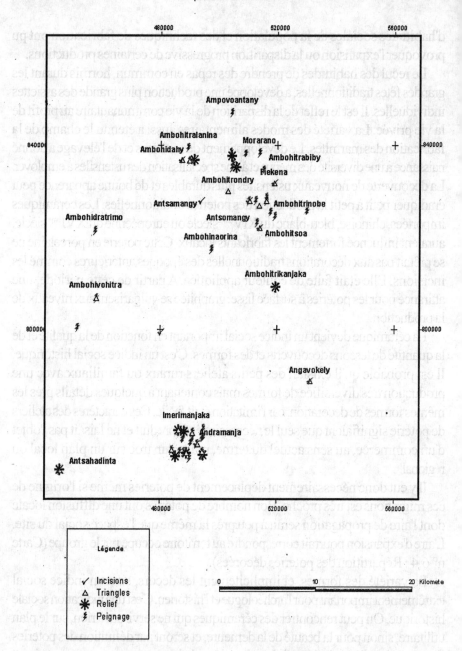

Carte n° 6.4 : *Répartition des poteries décorées*

CONCLUSION

Au terme de cette étude que nous avons menée, des réflexions se dégagent. La première concerne la répartition géographique des décorations sur les poteries de l'Imerina. Il sera encore difficile de connaître réellement et d'une manière absolue les origines de cette distribution. Malgré tout, des zones de densité de population, rayonnant autour des grands centres historiques, correspondent à une zone de densité de poteries décorées. La richesse de ces régions dénote-t-elle qu'une population aurait pu s'y installer très tôt, avant le peuplement des autres régions ? En tout cas, ces régions ont reçu à travers leur histoire une forte migration. Les migrations seraient dues à une expansion démographique ou à une conquête de terre dans le cadre d'une colonisation agricole. Les données archéologiques concernant ces périodes reculées sont encore insuffisantes pour affirmer ou apporter de nouvelles explications sur ce peuplement ancien des Hautes Terres centrales de l'Imerina.

La deuxième remarque est que la variation des décors peut servir à la délimitation de vastes groupes homogènes pour une région et pour une époque donnée. Les données en notre possession indiquent une certaine homogénéité des styles jusqu'à la phase Angavobe, deuxième moitié du XVIème siècle et première moitié du XVIIème siècle. Cette homogénéité reflète une concentration de la population sur des espaces (souvent isolés?), concentration provoquée par un début d'accroissement démographique et de déplacement de l'habitat. Cette situation a entraîné la consolidation de sites d'habitat par le renforcement des systèmes défensifs (Mille 1970).

La troisième remarque concerne la rupture ou la disparition d'un style de décoration. En effet, à partir de la phase Angavobe, une régression en quantité de poteries avec décoration est significative jusqu'à la phase Fiadanana, milieu du XIXème siècle. Les changements sociaux et économiques sont influents sur les genres de vie communautaire. Les modes d'acquisition des produits et leur finalité ont changé. Les relations de plus grande échelle, qui passent de la communauté à la région, ont dû modifier le processus traditionnel, reposant uniquement sur les besoins de la famille.

La production s'est adaptée au nouveau courant d'échange. Le style de décoration est donc resté un élément de différenciation des groupes ou plutôt des périodes où il a été créé.

BIBLIOGRAPHIE

Arnaud, R. (1970)
    "Les anciens villages fortifiés de l'Ambohimarina," Université de Madagascar. *Taloha* 3 : 113-126.
Barret, J.B. (1985)
    Sarodrano : Etude d'un site Archéologique du Sud Ouest Malgache, Paris :Université de Paris I (Panthéon-Sorbonne).
Darsot, R. (2001)
    "Les Décors Céramiques sur la Poterie Locale de l'Imerina Ancien." Les collections de l'Institut de Civilisations-Musée d'Art et d'Archéologie, Université d'Antananarivo, 105p.
Ferry, Cap. (Juin 1898)
    " La terre cuite dans la région de Tananarive," *Notes, Reconnaissances et Explorations* (T. III, 2ème année) : 717-732.
Kus,. S et Wright, H. T. (1986)
    "Survey Archéologique de la Région d'Avaradrano," Antananarivo, Université de Madagascar. *Taloha* 10 : 49-72.
Mantaux, C.G (1970)
    " Sites Fortifiés du XVIè au XIXè siècle," *Revue de Madagascar* 51 et 52 : 21-   49.
Rafolo, A. (1989)
    "Habitats Fortifiés et Organisation de l'espace dans le Vonizongo (Centre ouest de Madagascar) :le cas de Lohavohitra," Unpublished Thèse de Doctorat. Paris : Université de Paris I- Sorbonne. 481 p.
Rasamuel, D. (1984)
    "L'ancien Fanongoavana," Unpublished Thèse de Doctorat. Paris : Université de Paris I. 454 p.
Santrot, J. et M.H. (1979)
    Céramiques Communes Gallo-romaines d'Aquitaine, éd. C.N.R.S.
Vérin, P. (1968)
    " Notes sur Quelques Types de Poteries Désuets de Madagascar." *Asian Perspectives*.
Vérin, P. (1975)
    Les échelles anciennes du commerce sur les côtes nord de Madagascar, Lille : Service de Reproduction des Thèses. Tome I.
Wright, H.T. et alii. (1987)
    "Datation Absolue de Sites Archéologiques du Centre de Madagascar- Présentation des Déterminations," Université d'Antananarivo: Musée d'Art et d'Archéologie. *Taloha* 11 : 121-146.

Endnotes

[1] Nous citerons entre autres les travaux de Wright sur l'évolution de la poterie locale ancienne de l'Imerina, ceux de Rasamuel sur les analyses en laboratoire des poteries de l'Ancien Fanongoavana et les travaux de Vérin portant sur les anciens sites de la région d'Anjozorobe et de la Mananara.

2 Article publié par Ferry Cap. (juin 1898) traitant de "La terre cuite dans la région de Tananarive." *Notes, Reconnaissances et Explorations* (Tome III, 2ème année): 717-732.

3 Rasamuel, D. (1984) L'ancien Fanongoavana, Paris Université de Paris I : Thèse de Doctorat de 3ème cycle.

4 Wright, H.T. (1986) " Survey archéologique de la région de l'Avaradrano." Taloha 10 : 49-72.

5 Rice, M. P (1987). *Pottery Analysis*. The University of Chicago Press.

6 Santrot, M. H. et J. (1979) *La Céramique Gallo-romaine d'Aquitaine*, Paris: éd. CNRS..

7 Rasamuel, D. (1984) "L'Ancien Fanongoavana." Paris : Thèse de Doctorat.

8 Des travaux de fouilles archéologiques, en Septembre 2000, avec le Centre d'Art et 'Archéologie de l'Université d'Antananarivo ont Permis de Mettre au Jour un Petit Four Pour la Cuisson de Poteries.

9 Les travaux sur le site de Lohavohitra dans le Voninzongo ont révélé la présence de boules d'argile cuite qui ont servi à la fabrication.

10 Les *Sinibe* peuvent servir de contenant de denrées, comme le paddy. Nous avons rencontré ce cas lors des fouilles de sauvetage de Mahitsielafanjaka en 1996 dans le Rova d'Antananarivo. Ce mobilier était enfoui dans la partie nord-est de la case royale d'Andrianampoinimerina au Rova. Il était en outre décoré par des motifs en relief simple.

11 Il est plus facile de prendre et de manier un plat avec un bord plus étalé surtout si le contenu est chaud lors des repas. La forme prédestine à une décoration.

12 Le terme de localité se prête mieux pour désigner les sites d'habitat où des centres de production ont pu exister.

13 Le terme peut prêter à confusion car un objet a toujours une utilité. Cependant, le principe de fabrication de la poterie repose sur le critère pratique de son utilisation. La beauté n'est alors que secondaire

An Evaluation of the Critical Economic Resources of Great Zimbabwe, 1200 -1500 AD: A Preliminary Ethno-botanical Survey of Edible Wild Fruits

Edward Matenga

INTRODUCTION

Great Zimbabwe is an archaeological site with the remains of large dry stone buildings built and occupied by a Shona ruling elite between the 13th and 15th centuries. The stone walls crown the summit of a granite hill, the Zimbabwe Hill, rising 100 m above the adjacent valley. The ruin field spreads into the valley to the south covering some 250 hectares of land. The dry stonework forms enclosures which screened dwelling houses. It also retained platforms upon which houses were built. The stone buildings formed the core of the Great Zimbabwe settlement which otherwise was quite extensive. Presently 720 hectares is protected.

The spatial extent of Great Zimbabwe is clear testimony to the fact that during its time it was the largest settlement in Sub-Saharan Africa. The stone building tradition was practised mainly on the plateau between the Zambezi and Limpopo rivers (what is now the modern state of Zimbabwe) where more than two hundred and fifty sites are known to exist. A few more sites are found in parts of South Africa, Mozambique and Botswana which border on Zimbabwe (Figure 7.1).

Archaeological explorations in the 20th century yielded a large body of

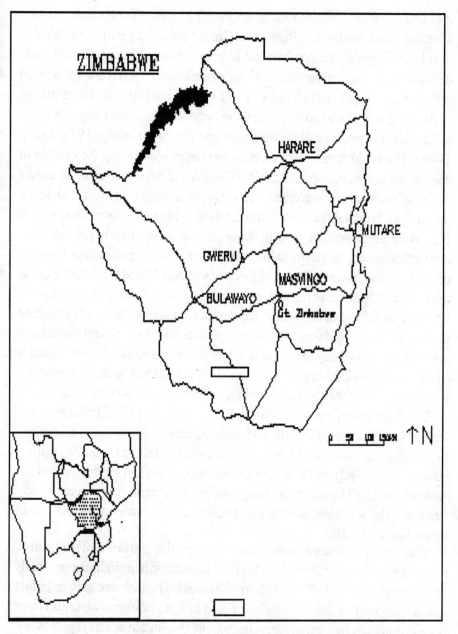

Fig. 7.1: *A map of Zimbabwe showing the location of Great Zimbabwe*

data which has been used to reconstruct the life history of the ancient site. Quite a lot, therefore, has been written about Great Zimbabwe's political control of the plateau between the Zambezi and Limpopo Rivers, its long-distance trade networking within the southern African region and with Asia through the East African coast (Sinclair 1987). The archaeological assemblage indicates that beef was an important component of the day-to-day diet of the ruling elite but not typical for the common citizenry (Garlake 1978; Thorp 1996). The inhabitants were crop farmers as evidenced by the finding of carbonised sorghum seeds on the Hill Complex. The largest population ever to live at the site has been estimated variously from 5,000 to 30,000. More than animal husbandry and agriculture, Great Zimbabwe's population utilised the environment around them in many other ways in order to provide their own subsistence. It is regrettable that to date no attempt has been made to reconstruct the entire spectrum of foods which constituted the dietary regime of the Great Zimbabwe inhabitants. A preliminary ethno-botanical survey, which is the subject of this article, has demonstrated that the Great Zimbabwe district today abounds with edible indigenous wild fruits which must have contributed immensely to the medicinal and vitamin needs of the inhabitants of the site. It will be argued that this data is vital to the study towards a reconstruction of the food archaeology of the Great Zimbabwe site.

The first botanical survey in the environs of Great Zimbabwe was undertaken in the early 1980's by J. H. Bannerman with the object of identifying the ecological factors which led to the rise and fall of Great Zimbabwe (Bannerman 1982). In 1998 a Swiss botanist, Mueller (1998), carried out another survey. The latter had longstanding experience of tropical woody flora since he was instrumental in the setting up of a National Herbarium in Harare in the 1960s.

The Great Zimbabwe exercise was for the purpose of providing recommendations for the reclamation and restoration of its indigenous woody vegetation (Mueller 1998:5). The survey revealed that the tree species before and during part of the occupation period of Great Zimbabwe could have been dominated by Brachystegia (msasa and mountain acacia) species and *Julbernardia globiflora*. These species are known to intermix with a wide range of trees with edible wild fruits. The dominant species mentioned above have been wiped out from the central area of the site. The trees with edible fruits also exist in numbers far less than normal and in certain cases they have been eliminated altogether. Part of the evidence that the vegetation configuration in the central area has changed is circumstantial: healthy colonies of the same species and the associated fruit trees thrive in an area less than 1.5 km from the centre of the site within the 720 hectares estate protected by a boundary fence. It is also an established fact that where dominant species have been eliminated they are replaced by various species of acacia which are indeed very aggressive colonists.

The main reason for the degradation of the woody flora in the central area of the site is thought to be exploitation of the woodland in ancient and modern times for firewood and timber. Over-exploitation of the environment is thought to have been responsible for the collapse of Great Zimbabwe in the 15th century. Seasonal bush fires in ancient and modern times certainly added to the toll. Richard Hall, the first Curator of Great Zimbabwe appointed in 1902, cleared large parts of the central area of trees supposedly to open the site and make it more attractive to tourists (Garlake 1973: 72). Furthermore during the last century, almost every year during the wet season the central area of the monument has been subjected to seasonal wholesale clearance of vegetation which precluded any regeneration.

RESEARCH OBJECTIVES AND METHODS

The primary focus of this preliminary ethno-botanical survey was the study and inventorying of fruit trees in the Great Zimbabwe district, an area of 25 km radius of the centre of the site. This was with a view to producing an inventory which could shed more light on the dietary regime of the inhabitants of Great Zimbabwe. In this preliminary study, the relative abundance of the fruit trees was assessed. While an evaluation of the nutritional value of wild fruits has to await further botanical analysis, preliminary information was obtained from existing literature and from field oral enquiries.

The research area was divided into three concentric zones around the centre of Great Zimbabwe, the centre being arbitrarily marked as the site museum.

Zone 1: 0 - 1 km radius of the centre of the Great Zimbabwe Estate
Zone 2: 1- 2 km radius of the centre of the Great Zimbabwe Estate
Zone 3: 2 - 25 km radius of the centre of the Great Zimbabwe Estate. A large proportion of Zone 3 is communal land.

In Zones 1 and 2 (the Great Zimbabwe Estate), straight-line walking surveys were conducted during which a species count was undertaken. A vehicle was used to survey Zone 3 using established roads. People were asked about the local significance of the trees. The informants volunteered information about fruit trees without any reservation. Some curious reticence was however observed when the subject of medicinal plants was raised. The practice of medicine in many parts of Africa is an esoteric profession and often overlaps with magical practices. Thus informants are usually not forthcoming. Using the above method, a reasonably representative sample of data on the ethno-botany of edible indigenous fruits was obtained.

Observations

A total of 32 trees with edible fruits was found in the Great Zimbabwe district. Of these, two species could not be identified with their botanical names. All the 32 fruit trees were found in Zone 3. This was indeed not surprising because the probability of finding all fruit trees in Zone 3 was in any case very high because it is a much wider area than Zones 1 and 2. 15 species were found in Zone 1 where all but one species (*Azanza garckeana*) occurred with less than normal populations when compared with populations in Zones 2 and 3. *Azanza garckeana*, and to a minor degree Sclerocarya caffra appear to have sufficient regenerative powers to defy the constraints existing in Zone 1. This is the only fruit tree which continues to grow in large numbers in the central area. This shows that the species was an easily renewable resource and the inhabitants of Great Zimbabwe could have sustained sufficient numbers around the site. 29 species were found in Zone 2, demonstrating that in spite of the constraints certain areas of the state have retained a population of the species which is fairly representative of the bio-diversity of the site in the ancient past. Three species occurred in Zone 3 alone, all of them confined to low-lying areas in the south-western fringe of the study area. Conspicuously absent in Zones 1 and 2 is the sweet flavoured fruit, *Uapaca kirkiana* (described below).

The study demonstrates that it is highly likely that those species occurring in Zone 2 were originally found in Zone 1. Their absence can be reasonably be deduced to be a function of environmental degradation which the central area has experienced in the last century.

The harvest times were analysed. Basically the fruit trees can be classified into wet and dry season harvests with a 56% to 44% ratio respectively. It was also observed that the individual harvest times in most cases either run concurrently or overlap. There is probably a four week gap around May which is yet to be confirmed.

Case Study of Main Species

1) The commonest fruit tree species in Zone 1, the central area, was *Azanza garckeana*. This is a scattered tree never dominant in any particular place but nevertheless dominant in terms of geographic spread. The tree seems to grow easily and the large numbers in the central area of the monument seem to reflect regeneration which has taken place in the last 50 years. This shows that this species was a renewable resource and therefore sustainable in ancient times.

2) The second commonest species in the Great Zimbabwe Estate is *Parinari curatellifolia* (hissing tree, *mobola* plum). This evergreen tree tends to form colonies but is also scattered. Zone 1 is now almost devoid of this tree. Our field experience is that it is prone to destruction during bush fires.

The *mobola* plum is much sought after by the rural folk and is often left standing in the fields. The fruit may be eaten fresh. The fruit flesh can also be made into a porridge. The rural folk ferment an intoxicating liquor from it. A medical remedy is extracted from the bark for the treatment of pneumonia. The crown of the tree gives an excellent shade. It is interesting to note that when the famous Scottish doctor and first European visitor to the Victoria Falls on the Zambezi River in 1855, David Livingstone, died in Zambia in 1873 a commemorative inscription was carved on the trunk of a fine mobola tree. The Shona of Zimbabwe hold traditional religious ceremonies under mobola trees.

3) An equally dominant but scattered tree is *Sclerocarya caffra* (commonly known as *marula*). This tree is spread throughout the Great Zimbabwe Estate and beyond. It is easy to regenerate from seeds and truncheons and this may explain its abundance in the reserve and the neighbouring district. The pulp is of tremendous nutritional value as it contains four times as much vitamin C as orange juice (Palgrave 1977: 458). The pulp is fermented into an intoxicating drink (*mukumbi*), a common practice in all parts of southern Africa. A hard globular shell contains two or three white seeds (nuts) the oil of which is rich in protein. The trunk can be carved into a mortar or drum. The bark is widely used in southern Africa in traditional medicine. Because elephants have a craving for the fruit and bark the tree is also called the elephant tree. There is a proverbial saying in the Shona language likening an unexpected encounter between two people in an odd place to the meeting of elephants at a marula tree.

Very few individuals of *Uapaca kirkiana* (*muhobohobo or muzhanje*), an otherwise very abundant fruit tree, can be seen in the Great Zimbabwe Estate today. We believe that in ancient times this was probably the most populous fruit tree in the area because it is has a tendency to form fairly dense monolithic colonies. But it is now confined to the eastern fringe of the Estate. However it is still very abundant elsewhere in the Great Zimbabwe district both as scattered trees interspersed with *Brachystegia* (*miombo*) and as colonies. Extensive colonies exist in the Morgenster Mission Farm immediately south of Great Zimbabwe and in the communal areas to the south-east of Great Zimbabwe. The sugary fruits which ripen in November-December, have become a modern delicacy and are harvested by vendors who sell them at roadside markets and even in the main urban centres of Harare and Bulawayo. Because of commercialisation of the fruit, rural communities have taken the initiative in preserving the tree. The fruit may be allowed to ferment into an intoxicating liquor. Hunters were known to loathe a muhobohobo bush because the crackling sound of the dry and brittle leaves scares away animals. On the other hand, the famous 19th century European traveller and painter, Thomas Baines (see Palgrave 1977: 408-409) remarked that in two or three hours it looses its cool, glossy green color. Baines, in his diaries, mentioned that the tree affords the best time test for it is when it is old it begins to look dry and pale.

4) *Ficus burkei* and *Ficus capensis*: The ficus genus has a large number of species and more than 30 have been identified in southern Africa. *Ficus capensis* is large tree rising up to 12 metres and the crown provides an excellent shade. The tree can easily be grown from truncheons. *Ficus burkei* is another species which occurs in the reserve. It is a very variable and widely distributed species. Like its sister species, *F. capensis,* it can easily be grown from truncheons.

5) Other species which are worthy of discussion here are two related species of Strychnos, i.e. *Strychnos cocculoides* and *Strychnos spinosa*. These trees are scattered and rarely occur close together. There is a modest population of these trees in the Great Zimbabwe Reserve. What is of particular interest is that in folklore, *S. spinosa* is presented as sweeter and hence more pleasant than the other species. This assertion is apparently a falsehood crafted to detract attention from *S. coccuoloides* which apparently has a more pleasant flavour.

DISCUSSION AND CONCLUSIONS

The story of Great Zimbabwe as presently described leaves a number of things unaccounted for, or perhaps taken for granted. This preliminary ethno-botanical survey has yielded data which can be used to reconstruct aspects of the diet of the inhabitants of Great Zimbabwe. It is an assumption which can be tested that many of the vitamins required by the site's residents were derived from edible wild fruits such as the Vitamin C in *marula* plum noted above. Furthermore a number of the edible fruits may have had medicinal value which the inhabitants used consciously or unconsciously. This ethno-botanical study has the potential to shed more light on the nutrition and health of the early inhabitants. Nutrition is a key determinant of demographic patterns. A good and stable nutritional regime lays the foundation for a healthy and vibrant population. This brings us to the question of human resources as a development resource and as such a factor in the rise and sustenance of the Great Zimbabwe state. This question has never been investigated. Yet it is know from modern experience that some systems are severely disabled if the appropriate human resources are not available, or if a healthy active population does not exist. Demographic factors such as population size, numbers in age groups, gender and public health were critical to the sustenance of a political system such as the Great Zimbabwe Estate. Yet they are largely dependent on the availability of essential food ingredients.

The above study has demonstrated that there are some perspectives on the history of the rise of the Great Zimbabwe state which have not be fully explored, e.g. the availability of food resources which has a bearing on nutrition and demographic patterns. Historians have sometimes uncritically given eminence to some theses such as the trade hypothesis to explain the rise and survival of the Great Zimbabwe polity (Huffman, 1972). While this ethno-botanical study of food is not being mooted as a counter-hypothesis, it shows that the sustenance of a complex agriculturally based political system is, strictly speaking, dependent on a wide range of factors, one of them being those ingredients such as food/vitamins necessary for the development of a sound human population base. This study thus presents an important finding which can stimulate further research on the various aspects of Great Zimbabwe's domestic economy.

REFERENCES

Bannerman, J. H. (1982)
"Ecological and Other Factors in the Rise and Fall of the Great Zimbabwe State." Paper presented in a conference on Zimbabwean History, University of Zimbabwe.

Drummond, R. B. & Palgrav,. K. C. (1973)
CommonTrees of the Highveld. Sàlisbury: Longmans.

Garlake, P. S. (1973)
Great Zimbabwe. London: Thames and Hudson.

Garlake, P. S. (1978)
"Pastoralism and Zimbabwe." *Journal of African History* 19 (4): 479-494.

Huffman, T. N. (1972)
"The Rise and Fall of Zimbabwe." *Journal of African History* 13 (3): 353-366.

Mueller, T. (1998)
"Proposal for Improving the Landscape of the Great Zimbabwe National Monument Estate." (Unpublished).

Palgrave, K. C. (1977)
Trees of Southern Africa. Cape Town: C. Struik

Sinclair, P. J. J. (1987)
Space, Time and Social Formation: A Territorial Approach to the Archaeology and Anthropology of Zimbabwe and Mozambique c. 0AD. -1700. Uppsala: Societas Arhaeologica Upsaliensis.

Thorp, C. R. (1996)
Kings, Commoners and Cattle at Zimbabwe Traditional Sites. Harare: National Museums and Monuments of Zimbabwe.

Wild, H. (undated).
A Rhodesian Botanical Dictionary of African and English Plant Names. Salisbury: Government Printers.

Shifting Patterns of Trade in the Western Indian Ocean Zone: Northern Zimbabwe, 1500-1750 AD

8

Innocent Pikirayi

INTRODUCTION

Prior to 1560 trade along the western Indian Ocean coast and adjacent hinterland territories of eastern Africa had been dominated by the Swahili. These had a longstanding history of settlement and commercial interaction with the whole East African coast from Sofala in Mozambique to the Somali coast in the Horn of Africa. Archaeological and historical evidence points to trading networks and contacts with the Far East, the Persian Gulf as well as India (Chaudhuri 1985, Kusimba 1999) based on interchange of goods between coastal entrepreneurs and commercial interests in the interior. The Portuguese, who arrived in the East African region just before 1500, established a system of captains on a number of forts adjacent to Swahili towns with the objective of taking over the commerce from the latter. They failed however to dictate the terms of trade, as they could not maintain a strong military presence in the region. The situation changed just after 1560, when an attempt to introduce Christianity in the interior seriously backfired, resulting in the murder of a Portuguese priest. This provided the Portuguese with an excuse to intervene militarily in the hinterland at the same time taking control of the gold trade. The gold trade became an aggressive commercial undertaking, which adversely affected some societies in the African hinterland.

The eighteenth century saw a return to trading patterns obtaining during the first half of the sixteenth century, after the expulsion of the Portuguese traders from parts of the interior. This chapter traces these dynamic trading patterns through careful examination of archaeological and historical evidence. It focuses on northern Zimbabwe and the adjacent regions of the lower Zambezi valley, once under the control and influence of the Mutapa state, established there during the middle of the fifteenth century. This came after the decline of a state centred at Great Zimbabwe, some 400 km to the south, of which it was a cultural and political successor.

EARLY SWAHILI-PORTUGUESE CONTACTS IN EASTERN AFRICA

When the Portuguese arrived on the East African coast early in 1498 they sought to control the trading markets of the Swahili towns, which had long-established commercial contacts with the hinterland. They were interested in the exchange of goods manufactured in Portuguese factories in Goa, India, for gold, as well as other commodities such as ivory available along trade routes leading to the heart of the continent. The history of this commercial interaction, prior to the coming of the Portuguese, is long and apparently prosperous, beginning with the growth of the towns of Schroda and Bambandyanalo in the middle Limpopo valley, which traded gold, ivory and animal skin in exchange for imported cloth and glass beads (Hanisch 1980). This trade is linked to the Swahili (Hall 1987), who relied on longstanding and extensive exchange networks, whereby they purchased goods at their markets for resale in remote hinterland villages. This would remain a thriving commercial interchange until the Portuguese and Arab conquests of the coastal towns that would result in the emergence of new patterns of trade on the East African coast during the sixteenth and seventeenth centuries (Chittick 1974, Kusimba 1999). The arrival of the Portuguese saw the occupation of strategic points along the Indian Ocean coast in an attempt to secure a stake in the maritime trade (Smith 1983). They soon learnt about the gold coming in from an African kingdom located somewhere in the interior. This was a plateau region south of the Zambezi, controlled by kings with a dynastic title "Monomotapa" or "Mwene Mutapa."

In order to control the gold trade, the Swahili had established the towns of Sofala and Angoche on the Mozambican coast, and these were operational when the Portuguese arrived in the maritime region at the beginning of the sixteenth century. Immediately after, the Portuguese anxiously gathered information about these gold mines. A Viceroy was later appointed in Goa charged with the responsibility of registering all merchandise sent from Portugal, and redistributing it to various factories including Sofala manned by captains and secretaries, who in turn traded with the local people. Sofala was particularly strategic, since it tapped the gold coming from the interior. For this to take place effectively, they had to know the location of mines, production, rates of exchange, the African rulers and their political systems. Local informants sometimes provided this information although the Portuguese sent their own fact-finding missions into the interior as in the case of Antonio Fernandes between 1505 and 1512 (Godlonton 1945). Forts were built at Sofala, Kilwa (Gereza) and Mozambique Island (near the Swahili town of Angoche) between 1505 and 1507 to forcibly control the gold trade coming from the Zimbabwe interior (Map 8.1). This was followed by an attack on, and occupation of, various Swahili towns so that by 1512 the Portuguese effectively dominated the western Indian Ocean coast (Smith 1983: 221). However, an attempt to monopolise the trade failed, as the Swahili merchants bypassed the Portuguese easily. During the late seventeenth century the northern cities of the East African coast came under Omani rule (Kusimba 1999), effectively reducing Portuguese influence. Controlling the Coast was one thing, Portugal was a maritime power, but the Portuguese had scanty knowledge of the interior, the source of the gold. Attempting to overcome this they decided to settle close to the centres of gold and ivory production and commerce. This brought them into the lower Zambezi valley and later into northern Zimbabwe, the heartland of the "Monomotapa" or "Mwene Mutapa" (referred to hereafter as the Mutapa State) (Map 8.2).

Another problem connected with the gold trade was political instability between coastal and hinterland rulers on the one hand and among some hinterland groups on the other over the control of the trade channelled to the coast of Mozambique. The rulers wanted a stake in the cloth and glass beads trade going inland from Sofala in exchange for the gold and ivory from the interior (Bhila 1983). The conflicts which were taking place at a time when the Portuguese were trying to settle permanently on the Mozambican coast

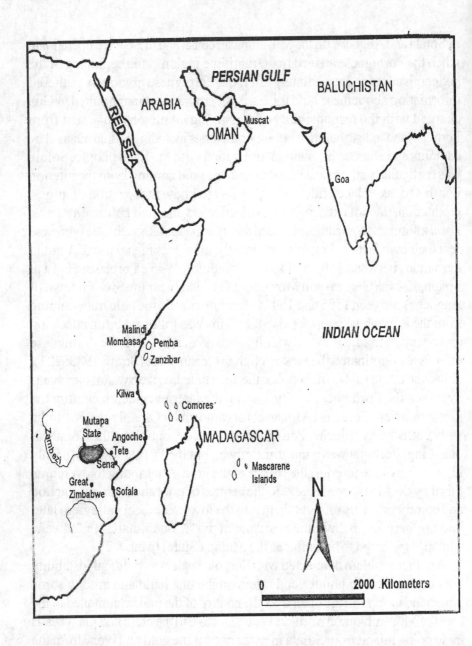

Map 8.1: *The Zimbabwe Plateau in relation to the Western Indian Ocean coast. The Mutapa state (1450-1900 AD) occupied the northern part of the plateau*

ERRATA: Plate 8.3 should read 8.2
Plate 8.4 should read 8.3

were responsible for the abandonment of Sofala in favour of the lower Zambezi valley towns of Sena and Tete during the 1530s. By 1541 some of the Portuguese were living in the lower Zambezi valley interior and were individually conducting trade (Beach 1980: 260).

The first attempts to directly influence and interfere with the politics of Mutapa state are seen in the introduction of Christianity at the court, a move strongly resented by the essentially Muslim Swahili traders. This led to the death of the priest, Fr. Goncalo da Silveira in 1561, whose murder provided the Portuguese with the excuse necessary to intervene militarily. The Portuguese saw an opportunity to expel Swahili traders from the Mutapa state that would then be followed by control of the gold mines, which the local rulers had to surrender. The military campaigns of 1569-75 attempted to conquer the Mutapa state from the lower Zambezi and the territory of Manyika in the east. It was clear from such campaigns that the Portuguese had decided to conduct their commerce aggressively. This created highly unstable political conditions in the lower Zambezi, in addition to the Zimba from Maravi, who were also attacking the region. The Mutapa state was also facing civil unrest which, during the early seventeenth century, the Portuguese took advantage of. Swahili trade and the Mutapa state declined and with these developments, the Portuguese were presented with an opportunity to set up trading settlements in the hinterland.

Feiras of 'Mukaranga'

Following the abortive military campaigns of 1569-75, the decline of the Swahili influence of the Mutapa state and the political instability in the interior, the Portuguese decided to move into northern Zimbabwe. Archaeological sites characterised by the presence of imported ceramics and beads attest to this development. These settlements, referred to in Portuguese documents as *feiras* (markets), provide tangible evidence of contact between the local communities and the European traders (Map 8.3). Most were built in areas under the control or influence of local rulers who had a stake in the trade. Local pottery identifies the indigenous communities with the people sharing the same culture system as Great Zimbabwe in the southern plateau, some 100 years before (Pikirayi 1997).

In the upper and middle sections of the Mazowe River valley archaeologists

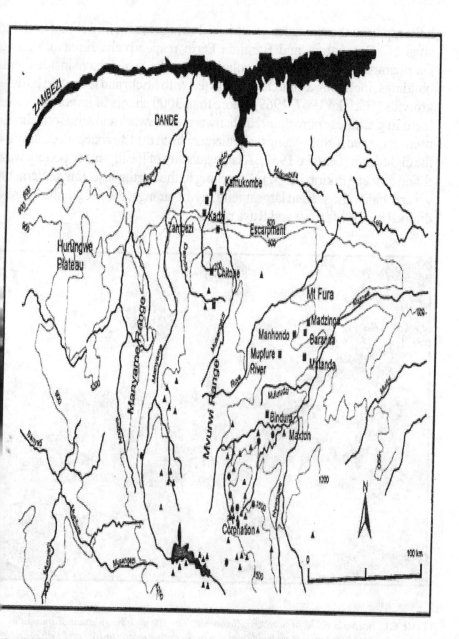

Map 8.3: *Some capital centres (in triangles) and African-Portuguese trading settlements (squares) in the Mutapa state, Northern Zimbabwe*

have reported the existence of African-Portuguese trading contacts at the sites of Dambarare and Baranda Farm respectively. Excavations at Dambarare exposed six rectangular earthworks, which have inside them buildings, including a church, constructed with brick; and Christian burial-grounds (Garlake 1967, 1969). More than 3000 sherds of imported ware, including Chinese porcelain, earthenware, stoneware and terracotta, have been recovered, firmly dating the settlement from the late sixteenth century to the eighteenth (Garlake 1969). A large quantity of locally-made pottery was found as well (Pikirayi 1997). According to the Portuguese, this settlement was probably the second largest feira in Mukaranga, the geographical area drained by the Mazowe and Ruya rivers.

Plate 8.1: *Baranda Field in northern Zimbabwe. The site yielded substantial quantities imported ceramics, glass beads and glassware dating mostly to 16th and 17th centurie Its location coincides with the trading centre of Massapa, mentioned in Portugues written records*

At Baranda Farm near Mt Fura is evidence of an extensive town measuring over a kilometre across (Plate 8.1). Its inhabitants used quantities of locally-produced artifacts and a wide range of imported ones; sixteenth and seventeenth century glass beads, Persian and Far Eastern pottery and glassware (Pikirayi 1993). Local pottery suggests that a Zimbabwe Culture community based in the heartland of the Mutapa State had extensive and lucrative trading connections with the Indian Ocean coast. Their prosperity was evidently derived from the auriferous Mukaradzi River, which cuts into a gold belt stretching towards the Mazowe, some forty kilometres to the east. Baranda Farm marks the location of the trading town of Massapa, mentioned in the sixteenth and seventeenth century Portuguese records.

Table 8.1: *Random surface collections of imported ceramics, Baranda and nearby farm*

Location	Stoneware	Earthenware	Porcelain	Glassware	Total	
Farms 4/5	4	1	37	0	42	
Farms 3/7	46	72	123	14	255	
Total	50	73	160	14	297	
%	17%	25%	54%	5%	100%	

Table 8.2: *Controlled surface collections of imported ceramics, Baranda, northern Zimbabwe*

5 x 5 m unit	Stoneware	Earthenware	Porcelain	Glassware	Total
5541/018/10	1				1
5541/020/72	1	1			2
5541/036/99	3	1	4		8
5541/037/54	1				1
5541/079/98	1				1
5542/378/08	8		3		11
5542/379/29		1	5		6
5542/379/67		5	1		6
5542/379/74		1	1		2
5542/379/90		11	3	1	15
5542/380/51	4	1	3	1	9

Table 8.2: *Continued....*

5542/380/58			1		1
5542/380/78			2		2
5542/380/84	3	2	1		6
5542/398/01				1	1
5542/399/90	1		1		2
5542/400/10	1	1			2
5641/001/43	1				1
5641/001/47			2		2
5641/002/44	1				1
5641/002/93		1			1
5641/361/05	1	1	1	1	4
5642/378/26			4	1	5
5642/379/46	1	3	1		5
5642/381/30			1		1
Total	28	29	34	5	96
%	29.2%	30.2%	35.4%	5.2%	100%

Table 8.3: *Excavated imported ceramics from Baranda Farm, northern Zimbabwe*

Pit/Trench	Stoneware	Earthenware	Porcelain	Glassware	Total
Pit 1	1	1			2
Pit 3	2	4			7
Pit 4		1		1	2
Pit 5			1		1
Pit 7	5				5
Pit 8				2	2
Pit 9	1	1			2
Pit 16		1			1
Pit 17			1	1	2
Pit 28			2		2
Pit 29	2		1	1	4
Pit 33			2		2
Pit 43		1			2
Pit 44			1		1
Pit 45			1		1
Pit 46		1			1
Pit 48	1				1
Pit 50			1	1	2
Trench 1/1a	11	22	38	13	84
Total	23	32	48	19	124
%	18.5%	25.8%	38.7%	15.3%	100.0%

Table 8.4: Excavated glass beads from Baranda sorted primarily according to colour

Context	Indian red	light blue	dark blue	green	yellow	black	white	other
Pit 1	22	6	3	3				
Pit 2	60	2	3	3	4	1		
Pit 3	62	9	11		5	1		
Pit 4	43	8	2	5	5			
Pit 5	9	1	2	2				
Pit 6	4		1	1				
Pit 7	6		2	1				
Pit 8	44	15	6	4	8	1		
Pit 9	25	1	1	1	1			
Pit 10	18	1	3					
Pit 11	11		1					
Pit 12	10							
Pit 15	11	4	2					
Pit 16	16	9	2	2	4			
Pit 17	26	7	3	2	3	2		
Pit 18	70	4	1	2	2			
Pit 19	10							
Pit 20	4			1				
Pit 21	2	1						
Pit 22	5							
Pit 24	1		1					
Pit 25	4	1	1		1			
Pit 26	5	1						
Pit 27	40	2	3	7	2			
Pit 28	147	15	33	18	14	1		2
Pit 29	6							
Pit 30	36	2	4	2	4	1		
Pit 31	1							
Pit 32	10		1					
Pit 33	1							
Pit 36	1				1			
Pit 37	1							
Pit 38			2					
Pit 42	35	12	2	1	2	1	2	
Pit 43	301	6	31	5	10	1	1	
Pit 44	14	8	4	3	1			
Pit 45	15	8	7	2	4	5		

Table 8.5: *Dating of imported wares from Baranda: surface and excavated collections*

Period	Stoneware	Earthenware	Porcelain	Glassware	Total
15th century or earlier					0
15th century or later	62	31			93
16th-17th century	5		3		8
16th-early 17th century	1				1
16th-late 17th century		14	1		15
16th or 17th century			10		10
late 16th century			6		6
late 16th or early 17th centur	2	6	1		9
late 16th or late 17th century				1	1
late 16th-early 18th century			7		7
late 16th-late 17th century	1				1
17th century	2	1	63		66
17th or 18th century	1		15	5	21
late 17th-early 18th century			2		2
18th century			1		1
18th or 19th century			1		1
undated	34	100	142	32	308
Total	108	152	252	38	550

These documents say the town was in Mukaranga, the heartland of the Mutapa state (dos Santos in Theal 1898-1903 vol.7: 270-3). So important was this centre that the Portuguese appointed a resident, entitled Captain of the Gates, to live there permanently. He supervised the Portuguese traders operating in Mukaranga and negotiated trade alliances with the king (Theal 1898-1903 vol. 3 : 354, 271-2). So large was Massapa that it possessed a church similar to that at Dambarare (Theal 1898-1903 vol. 2: 438). Massapa is also mentioned in Portuguese accounts of civil wars that wracked the Mutapa state in the early seventeenth century. It was probably the biggest trading settlement in Mukaranga. Excavations and surface collections at Baranda Farm yielded substantial quantities of imported ceramic, beads and glassware (Pikirayi 1993: 75-83). Identification of the various imports found on the sites was done at Mombasa with the assistance of the late Dr Richard Wilding (Wilding 1989, 1991). These results are summarised in Tables 1 through 5.

In the north-eastern region of Zimbabwe, and close to the confluence of the Nyadiri and Ruenya rivers, are the *feiras* of Luanze and Bokuto (Garlake 1967). Luanze is dated in Portuguese records from 1850 to 1680, after which it was abandoned. It is about one and half kilometres across, with two rectangular earthworks, each with a banh and ditch, forming the centre of thr settlement. One of the earthworks had evidence of circular houses inside its banks.A stone built enclosure is situated immediately east of one of the earthworks. The area in between has up to 30 burials, none of which has been excavated. Garlake (1967) identified a rectangular pole and *dhaka* (clayey plaster) structure to the north of the earthworks as a Portuguese church. Excavations produced glazed and imported ware, glass beads, gold dust and pellets, and locally made pottery. The imported pottery confirms the dating given in Portuguese written sources. Bokuto, described by the Portuguese as a market, and located somewhere in the confluence region of the Mazowe and Nyadiri rivers (Axelson 1964), has not yet been identified archaeologically.

A number of trading centres to regions west of the Mutapa State suggest that trade from the Indian Ocean might have been channelled into the area through the Manyame-Angwa basin, during the middle to the later part of the seventeenth century. Sherds of blue-on-white porcelain have been found in one of the six rectangular earthworks situated in the upper Angwa valley. The chocolate glazed exterior is typical of the porcelain manufactured from the late seventeenth century to the eighteenth century (Garlake 1967, 1969). The single rectangular earthwork in the upper Mupfuri valley, Maramuca (or Rimuka), like the upper Angwa valley earthworks, had a rectangular brick building built inside. It is dated from the 1660s to the 1680s. The brown and black glazed Chinese stoneware jars of the late seventeenth century and glass beads are identical to those found at Dambarare and Luanze. There is little historical detail pertaining to the feiras of Chitomborwizi and Urupande, in the upper Manyame valley, and to the north of Maramuca, but it would appear that they were part of the trading system in the western regions of the state which developed following the decline of Luanze, Dambarare and Massapa.

Articulation of *Feira* Trade

There is no evidence on how the feiras operated during the sixteenth century. What is clear though is that traders from Sena and Tete on the Zambezi travelled to the gold-producing areas in Manyika and Mutapa on the Zimbabwe plateau. *Capitao-mores* (Portuguese administrative authorities) based there distributed merchandise to the traders who then took it further into the interior in exchange for gold and other valuables. This operation was not very different from the feira system in Portugal. African rulers probably protected the traders in return for some gifts. By the late sixteenth century, this system of trade was fully operational, but was also breeding new tensions. The traders were not always following the local laws and customs (Bhila 1983: 68).

Feiras in Mukaranga as well as Manyika to the east and Butua, a kingdom further to the west, were located in gold-rich regions, where traders met periodically to exchange their merchandise for gold and ivory. The initial choice of a place to conduct trade largely depended on the first traders to arrive in the interior as well as the amount of trade goods coming from the local population. Permanent settlements soon grew around these points of commercial contact, where business went on throughout the year, but at different levels of intensity depending on whether it was the harvest season or not. The existence of a Portuguese garrison in most *feiras* clearly showed these institutions were operating in foreign territory, and security considerations were paramount. People from local and distant regions thronged these *feiras* to trade in gold and ivory as well as food (see Bhila 1983: 72-7). By the early seventeenth century, *feiras* had become an integral part of the economic and social fabric of northern Zimbabwe societies.

Consequences of *Feira* Trade

From 1624 onwards, the Portuguese were supporting puppet aspirants to the Mutapa throne, and in 1629 resulted in the appointment of Kapararidze as king. He was forced to sign a treaty giving the Portuguese estate- (*prazo*) holders increased presence in the state and unlimited access to the gold mines. The subsequent creation of Portuguese militias unleashed violence onto the population and forcibly accessed gold mining areas through *feiras* in the Angwa valley, Rimuka, Urupande and Chitomborwizi areas. The bank and ditch structures described in connection with some of these centres were probably erected around this time. This was the ultimate price to pay for the gold which was found in the state, a situation that went on until the 1660s.

From ordinary trading points, as was the case during the early seventeenth century, *feiras* had been transformed into some form of fortification in order to protect the lucrative gold trade. The solution lay in the revival of a strong political authority that would confine the Portuguese traders to the feiras. This was partly achieved by king Mukombwe, but after the 1660s the state had already lost the territory of Mukaranga, its political heartland, and most Portuguese traders had retreated to the lower Zambezi due to local resistance and disease.

The Portuguese were eventually expelled from northern Zimbabwe during the 1690s. This expulsion forced an end to violent Portuguese trading practices and ushered in a return to pre-seventeenth century trading patterns. The Portuguese were restricted to the coast and river ports, where they had to employ African agents to conduct trade in the interior. Some feiras remained operational through the eighteenth century. Dambarare was re-opened sometime after 1720 and remained operational until 1750 (Mudenge 1988). The trade with the Rozvi further to the south-west meant a revival of a number of the *feiras* in the western regions in the eighteenth century. The Portuguese, now based at Zumbo, on the confluence of the Zambezi and Luangwa, used the Manyame-Angwa basin to gain entry into northern and north-western Zimbabwe (Garlake 1969).

Largely missing from the written accounts is the development of stone-walled fortifications. Over 100 such sites have been identified in the middle Mazowe River valley (Map 8.4). The settlements are peculiarly sited and part of a regional settlement pattern that is out of character with other settlements in the region. It appears that, following the decline of elite stone-building activity and the trading centres in the heartland of the Mutapa state, stone buildings with loopholes appeared (Plate 8.2). These structures are irregular, semi-circular or oval, the plan often dictated by the hilltop or mountain slope onto which they are built. The enclosures vary in size with diameters ranging from 30 to 50 m and enclosing interiors of between 700 and 7000 m^2, which would adequately accommodate several pole and dhaka houses. The walls were raised using undressed stones set in rough, irregular and uneven dry mortar coursing. The walls, which have an average height of about a metre, have an average thickness of half a metre. They rest on either rock or earth foundation, have no decoration, but most have small, square to rectangular openings. These loopholes average 20 cm2 and are often built at a height of between 40 and 50 cm above the wall foundation. The numbers of these openings vary from place to place, some enclosures having none, others as many as 5 or 6. Some sites have 13 to 18 loopholes. Apparently the higher the hill, the less accessible the settlement and the fewer loopholes required. The openings were used as peep holes, but written sources referring to the lower Zambezi mention their use as firing points by the locals against the Portuguese. The locals used wooden stockades (chuambos) as forts (see Theal 1898-1903, vol. 1: 37-40; vol. 3: 361-7). The population dynamics of northern Zimbabwe following the loss by the Mutapa state of the plateau region is poorly understood. However communities who were allocated portions of the depopulated land by king Mukombwe could have built such fortifications to protect themselves from the Portuguese (Pikirayi 1993: 182-5).

Plate8.2: *One of the loopholed stone structures located on the summit of Mt. Fura, in norther⌐ Zimbabwe. Excavations at Chenguruve and Munyekayawa hills tentantively date thes⌐ fortified settlements from the middle of the 17th century.*

Excavations conducted at Muchekayawa and Chenguruve hills in th⌐ Mukaradzi-Gwetera valleys (Map 8.4) reveal evidence of long-distance trad⌐

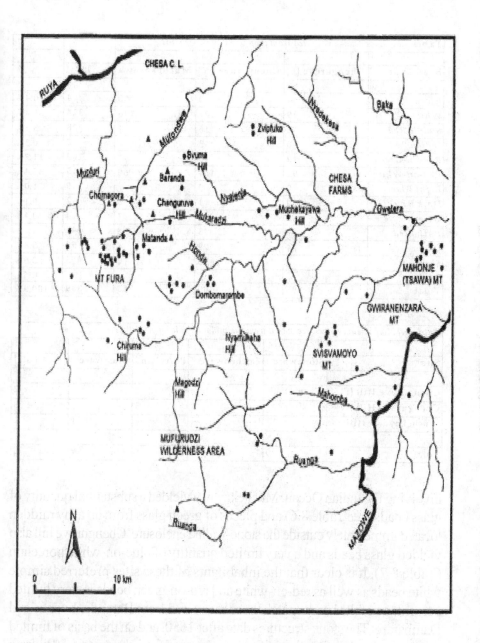

Map 8.4: *Distribution of loopholed stone strctures in the middle Mazowe basin, northern Zimbabwe.*

Table 8.6: *Glass beads excavated from loopholed stone structures*

Bead Type	Chenguruve [E]	Chenguruve [W]	Muchekayawa	Total	%
Black	4	0	0	4	0.4%
White	49	127	148	324	36.4%
Simple Red	8	16	4	28	3.1%
Indian Red	0	3	0	3	0.3%
Red-on-Green	12	45	47	104	11.7%
Red-on-White	91	164	60	315	35.4%
Light Blue	0	2	7	9	1.0%
Dark Blue	0	1	0	1	0.1%
Green	1	0	3	4	0.4%
Patinated	9	23	8	40	4.5%
Copper	24	22	6	52	5.8%
Shell	0	5	0	5	0.6%
Total	198	408	283	889	100.0%

Table 8.7: *Imported ceramics recovered from the middens of loopholed stone structures*

Site	Stoneware	Earthenware	Porcelain	Glassware	Total
Chenguruve Hill (E)			2		2
Chenguruve Hill (W)			3		3
Muchekayawa Hill				1	1
Total	0	0	5	1	6

involving the Indian Ocean. Muchekayawa yielded a substantial quantity of glass beads (see Table 8.6) and pieces of green glass from an ashy midden located immediately outside the stone-walled enclosure. Chenguruve hill also yielded glass beads and a very limited quantity of blue-on-white porcelain (Table 8.7). It is clear that the inhabitants of these sites preferred simple white beads as well as red-on-white and red-on-green beads. A very limited percentage of the beads match those recovered from Baranda, Luanze and Dambarare. The stone structures date after 1650, and on the basis of limited surface and subsurface deposits were occupied for a short period (Pikirayi 1993: 166-7). Clearly the patterns of trade with the Indian Ocean coast had changed by the middle of the seventeenth century and the emergence of fortified hilltop settlements points towards the highly insecure nature involved in the conduct of the trade. Although documents do not mention these stone-walled structures, their interpretation is consistent with the archaeological evidence.

INTERPRETING THE PATTERN FROM THE ARTIFACTS

The changing patterns of coast-interior trade as seen in northern Zimbabwe is largely due to the arrival of the Portuguese which ushered in European traders to the western Indian Ocean zone. Although the trade dominated by the Swahili can be considered a form of global exchange, European mercantilism was more aggressive and consequently ushered in violence which had a negative impact on some African social formations. In order to understand the nature and level of contact that took place between the Zimbabwe plateau and the coast during the period in question, it is necessary to discuss some of the assemblages recovered from excavations conducted in northern Zimbabwe. The global nature of trade linking northern Zimbabwe with the Indian Ocean is clearly mirrored in the ceramic and bead assemblages recovered from the sites.

The artifacts recovered at Baranda show a wide range of wares including porcelain, of Near Eastern and Chinese origin. This confirms a long traditional link between eastern Africa and the northern zones of the Indian Ocean. The bulk of the Chinese blue-on-white pottery in most areas of eastern Africa has been found on surface and upper occupation levels of sites, post-dating the coming of the Portuguese. This is reinforced by Wilding (1991) who points out that it was the Portuguese and later the Dutch who initiated the bulk transportation of Chinese wares to the Indian Ocean. The major part of this material, as the tables would indicate, was blue-on-white ware. The ware, according to Wilding, "was very common all over the Indian Ocean coast world, wherever Portuguese ships went...It is proper to make a direct association between the presence of large quantities of blue and white vessels and Portuguese trading influence."

The majority of wares from northern Zimbabwe are porcelains (Tables 1, 2, and 3). The region was firmly integrated into the Indian Ocean trading network slightly later than most parts of eastern Africa, and the fame of the gold from the interior played a considerable part in this development. It would appear that as from the fourteenth century onwards this route was broadened to include southern Africa and Europe and this could be explained by the arrival in the late fifteenth century of Portuguese traders in the Indian Ocean. This ensured the continued existence of the marine network through which ceramics were distributed, despite the restrictions imposed by the Chinese government at the end of the fourteenth century and the arrival in 1498 of the Portuguese in the Indian Ocean (Wilding, pers. com). Clearly therefore, Indian Ocean trade had become global in character.

When the Portuguese came to East Africa they altered the trading patterns between China and the Persian Gulf by channelling Far Eastern pottery through Goa in India rather than Kalah in the Malay Peninsula (Whitehouse 1973). This however did not stop the flow of wares from the Gulf, which during the fifteenth and sixteenth centuries increased significantly. The Portuguese were thus unable to impose a monopoly of the trade coming from both the Gulf and the Far East. What they only succeeded in doing was putting India in a firmer position as far as contacts with eastern African trade were concerned. Of the imported ceramic and glassware items recovered from Baranda Farm in northern Zimbabwe, 66.9% came from China and the Far East, mostly in the form of blue-on white porcelain, 18.7% came from the Persian Gulf area, 8.2% from Europe (Iberian wares), 2.5% came from either Europe or the Gulf, while the remaining 5.6% could not be positively identified in terms of place of origin. However the dominance of the Portuguese in the western Indian Ocean trade that involved the northern Zimbabwe plateau during the sixteenth and seventeenth centuries cannot be denied. While the dating of the wares is problematic (see Table 4), most of them were brought into northern Zimbabwe during the sixteenth or seventeenth centuries.

Earlier Chinese wares were an integral part of the silk trade. Silk was a highly prized commodity in constant demand all over the Indian Ocean zone. Chinese ceramics, especially the much earlier porcelain, are considered to be a visible, archaeological manifestation of this transoceanic enterprise, which also included incense, spices, medicinal plants, aromatics and precious stones (Sersterens 1985: 284). Poorly preserved cloth has been recovered in northern Zimbabwe (Garlake 1968, Huffman 1971). Cloth is also mentioned in

Portuguese documents referring to the Mutapa state in northern Zimbabwe and whose rulers highly valued the commodity. Thus in addition to ceramics and glass beads the Portuguese included silk in their trading operations in the India Ocean.

The Portuguese did not trade as many wares from the Persian Gulf and the Near East compared with Chinese ones mainly because they did not manage to control the trade coming from the region and they did not establish a long-term presence there. This is largely reflected in the relatively low frequency of Islamic wares found in northern Zimbabwe. In addition, the Gulf and the Near East experienced an economic decline during the sixteenth and seventeenth centuries resulting in the dispersal of potters to places like Turkey, Tunisia and Egypt. European influence in the region remained relatively weak until the middle or late eighteenth century when cheap European faience and porcelain reached there in large quantities, causing a decline in both Islamic and Chinese pottery (Richard Wilding, *pers. com.*).

Beads have been traded in the Indian Ocean Zone for over two thousand years (Chami 1999, 2002). Swahili merchants carried the bead trade along the western Indian Ocean coast as far as Sofala and the hinterland as far as the Zimbabwe plateau and the adjacent Shashe-Limpopo basin before the coming of the Portuguese (Hanisch 1980; Hall 1987; Wood 2002). Southern India is important in any discussion of the Indian Ocean trade network as is shown by Sher (1987: 181-99; Wood 2002). Some important Indian sites involved in the bead trade were Chanhudaro, Cambay, Poona, Brahamapuri, Goa, Arikamedu and Nagapatam. J. B. Lavanha's account of the wreck of the St Albert in 1593 states that beads of all colours were made in India at Nagapatam and exported to Mozambique. Particular mention is made of red beads worn by the Africans (Theal 1898-1903 vol. 2:. 303). Trade to southern and eastern Africa was facilitated by the ocean wind systems that involved the Monsoon and Trade Winds, so much so that the beads from India are sometimes referred to as 'trade-wind beads'. The glass beads recovered from the trading settlements at Dambarare, Massapa, Luanze and others suggest that glass beads were a popular item of trade during the sixteenth and seventeenth centuries. The popularity of the beads varied from region to region. However, the Indian Reds are regarded as the common trade beads, associated with the coming of the Portuguese and their subsequent attempts to wrestle the western Indian Ocean trade from the Swahili. According to Bhila (1983: 82), the popularity of the black, yellow, green-blue varied from region to region, but the commonest and most preferred beads were made in red and black. These were the Cambay beads and were preferred in all regions of Zambezia. Bead preference was determined by a set of beliefs common among the southern Zambezian states, including the Mutapa, Manyika and Torwa. The people believed that the Portuguese plucked these from trees, the black ones having been petrified as a result of being left on the trees for a long time, the green having been harvested before ripening, the red ones having been harvested on ripening, while the yellow ones had been removed just before ripening. Smaller beads were preferred compared to the large ones: they were in greater demand and highly priced.

The material recovered from Baranda Farm in northern Zimbabwe confirms the pattern as presented in the historical sources (Table 5). More than 74% of the glass beads were of the Indian red variety. Over 89% of the beads recovered at Baranda were classified in the small (2-4 mm) category and there were hardly any beads larger than this (Pikirayi 1993: 156). The artifacts clearly confirm the dominance of the Portuguese in western Indian Ocean trade during the sixteenth and seventeenth centuries. However, the beads recovered from the loopholed stone structures suggest a radical shift in the preference for glass beads as from the 1650s onwards (Table 8.6). If the information given in the written sources is anything to go by, then there was a disruption of the trade that was once dominated by the Portuguese. This is discussed below.

PATTERNS OF TRADE: 1650-1750

The archaeological record suggests that with the decline of the Portuguese presence on the Zimbabwe plateau patterns of trade changed after 1650. This aspect is vaguely reflected in the Portuguese written sources many of which refer to the lower Zambezi where they were establishing landed estates (*prazos*). This was probably due to a number of events which were taking place in the western Indian Ocean maritime sphere that effectively disrupted trade via the Gulf, India and the Far East. Slave trade is one possibility coupled with the arrival of the Dutch and later the British who posed a greater threat to the Portuguese traders.

The wars of the seventeenth and eighteenth century in the Mutapa state destroyed royal regulation in the conduct and operation of the trade and instead saw increased individual participation in the long-distance trade but on a reduced scale, which could have impacted the profitability of the enterprise. This is suggested by the evidence from the fortifications on Muchekayawa and Chenguruve hills in northern Zimbabwe where the glass beads differ significantly in terms of range and frequency (Table 8.6). Simple white beads dominate the assemblages of these sites, but also important are compound beads (red-on-white and red-on-green beads). Copper beads are also found but these vary significantly from site to site and were probably manufactured locally. The light blue, dark blue, green, Indian red and black oblates match those recovered at Baranda but they do not exceed 2% from any of the excavated assemblages. The enclosures at Chenguruve hill also yielded a few pieces of imported seventeenth century blue-on-white porcelain, clearly suggesting that there were no more direct contacts with the Far East after 1650. It is not easy to locate the source of some of these imports but they could have come from Europe given the increased European presence in the western Indian Ocean. Quantitatively, even if you consider the more than 100 fortified stone enclosures found in the middle Mazowe valley, it seems less imports arrived in northern Zimbabwe after 1650 than before.

CONCLUSIONS

Artifacts, in this case imported ceramic ware and glass beads, tell an interesting story spanning two and a half centuries about some of the trade involving African hinterland communities with the western Indian Ocean coastal towns. What is critical about the period 1500-1750 is the arrival onto the scene of Europeans, who attempted to globalise the entire Indian Ocean maritime trade, which also involved the Persian Gulf and lucrative markets in the Far East. Their contact with African rulers and populations resulted in a new set of relationships, which also affected the articulation and complexity of long-distance commerce. Northern Zimbabwe went through violent episodes following direct contact with the Portuguese traders during the sixteenth and seventeenth centuries. The archaeological pointers to this contact are in the form of changing artifact types, the emergence of trading centres and the appearance of fortified hilltop settlements. Here archaeology confirms the accounts presented in the documentary sources, but as in the case of the hill forts whereby the documents portray only a violent scenario, archaeology greatly amplifies the story. For the Mutapa state in northern Zimbabwe the ultimate price for actively participating in long-distance commerce with communities from the Indian Ocean coast was its demise, as these generated unstable political conditions at court. The period up to 1750 mainly shows how the shifting patterns of long-distance commerce affected the political process in northern Zimbabwe. Future research should amplify or modify some of the main issues presented here. Besides, there is also the acculturation process which comes about as a result of the introduction of the prazo system in the lower Zambezi. By the second half of the eighteenth century the Mutapa state had become much smaller in size, had adapted itself militarily to the activities of the Portuguese who were living in the Zambezi valley and thus managed to resist external threats. How this affected eighteenth and nineteenth century patterns of trade involving the lower Zambezi and the Indian Ocean remains a strong challenge for researchers.

REFERENCES

Axelson, F. (1964)
   The Portuguese in South Africa, 1600-1700. Johannesburg: Witwatersrand University Press.
Beach, D. N. (1980)
   The Shona and Zimbabwe, 900-1850: an Outline of Shona History. Gweru: Mambo Press.
Bhila, H. H. K. (1982)
   Trade and Politics in a Shona Kingdom: The Manyika and Their Portuguese and African Neighbours. Harare: Longmans.
Chami, F. (1999)
   "Roman Beads From the Rufiji Delta, Tanzania. First Incontrovertible Link with Periplus." *Current Anthropology* 40 (2): 237-241.
Chami, F. (2002)
   "People and Contacts in the Ancient Western Indian Ocean Seaboard or Azania." *Man and Environment* 27 (1): 33-44.
Chaudhuri, K. N. (1985)
   Trade and Civilisation in the Indian Ocean: an Economic History from the Rise of Islam to 1750. Cambridge: Cambridge University Press.

Chittick, N. (1974)
   Kilwa: An Islamic Trading City on the East African Coast, vol. 2. Nairobi: British Institute in Eastern Africa.
Garlake, P. S. (1967)
   "Seventeenth Century Portuguese Earthworks in Rhodesia." *South African Archaeological Bulletin* 21 (84): 157-70.
Garlake, P. S. (1969)
   "Excavations at the Seventeenth Century Portuguese Site of Dambarare." *Proceedings and Transactions of the Rhodesia Scientific Association* 54 (1): 23-61.
Godlonton, W. A. (1945)
   "The Journeys of Antonio Fernandes - the First Known European to Find Monomotapa and to Enter Southern Rhodesia." *Transactions of the Rhodesia Scientific Association* 11: 71-103.
Hall, M. (1987)
   The Changing Past: Farmers, Kings and Traders in Southern Africa. Cape Town: David Philip.
Hanisch, E. O. M. (1980)
   "An Archaeological Interpretation of Certain Iron Age Sites in the Limpopo-Shashe Valley." *M.A.* Thesis, University of Pretoria.
Huffman, T. N. (1971)
   "Cloth from the Iron Age in Rhodesia." *Anoldia* 5 (14): 1-7.
Kusimba, C. (1999)
   The Rise and Fall of Swahili States. Walnut Creek, London and New Delhi: Altamira Press.
Mudenge, S. I. G. (1988)
   A Political History of Munhumutapa. Harare: Zimbabwe Publishing House.
Pikirayi, I. (1993)
   "The Archaeological Identity of the Mutapa State:Ttowards an Historical Archaeology of Northern Zimbabwe." *Studies in African Archaeology* 6. Uppsala: Societas Archaeologica Upsaliensis.
Pikirayi, I, (1997)
   "The Pottery of the Historical Mutapa State: an Examination of the Local Ceramics from Some Trading Centres in Northern Zimbabwe." *Zimbabwea* 5: 30-47
Sersterens, M. P. (1985)
   "The Ceramic Route." In Beazely, M. (ed.); *The World Atlas of Archaeology*. Boston: G. K. Hall: 284-5.
Sher, D. L. (1987)
   The History of Beads From 3000 BC to the Present. New York: Hary N. Abrahams Inc. Publishers.
Smith, A. K. (1983)
   "The Indian Ocean Zone." In Birmingham. D. and Martin, P. M (eds), *History of Central Africa* Vol.1, 205-44. London and New York: Longman.
Theal, G. M. (1898-1903)
   Records of South Eastern Africa (in 9 volumes). Cape Town: C. Struik.

Whitehouse, D. (1973)
"Chinese Stoneware From Siraf: The Earliest Finds." *South Asian Archaeology* 10: 240-55.
Wilding, R. (1991)
"Dictionary of Ceramic Terms." Mombasa: The Library of Richard Wilding, unpublished.
Wilding, R. (1989)
"The Shorefolk: Aspects of the Early Development of Swahili Communities." Fort Jesus, Mombasa: *Occasional Papers* No. 2.
Wood, M. (2002)
"The Glass Beads of Kaole." In Chami, F. and Pwiti, G., (eds), *Southern Africa and the Swahili World*, 50-65. Studies in the African Past 2. Dar-es-Salaam: Dar-es-Salaam University Press.

9

Exploring Gender in Tiv Material Culture: Ethno-archaeology in the Katsina-Ala Valley

C. A. Folorunso

INTRODUCTION

It should be admitted that archaeologists continue to be very versatile and innovative in the way they produce knowledge from their data. However, a quick survey of some literature on the subject of gender study in archaeology may not reveal anything extraordinarily different from what had been the practice in archaeology in the past. Probably what is different is the call for more emphasis on extricating data that deal with gender and also to state explicitly what had been stated in general terms in the past. This is not a critique of gender archaeology in itself but to simply acknowledge the fact that the study of gender in archaeology is not completely new. The current emphasis on gender in archaeology would not be unconnected with the recognition that is generally accorded gender studies in the Social Sciences.

The specific consideration of gender in the archaeology data should be taken seriously because it would enrich our understanding of the past. It had been the practice of many people to equate gender with sex. However, an understanding of gender studies would show that gender is not the same as sex. Sex is the biological classification of male and female while gender is socially constructed (Nelson 1997). Sex and gender are commonly used, rightly or wrongly, to define people, their relationships to others and their place in society. The distinction of the sexes is usually based on observable biological traits, the genitalia. However, the emergence of sex change operations has complicated the biology of sexual division, and in this instance we have to deal with the question of the relative importance of the mind and the body (Hays-Gilpin and Whitley 1998:3)

In sex classification there are bound to be different specifics of sex categories among the different cultures. Biologically, there may be persons with female genital organs but who have no well-formed breasts, do not menstruate, or are totally barren. There may also be persons with male genital organs but who are impotent or have been castrated. All these are viewed differently from one culture to another and they may belong to different sex categories. Though sex is biological, sex categories are socially defined. Gender, which is defined as the cultural values inscribed on sex categories varies even more than sex. Gender categories have been the object of debate among political and religious factions (Hays-Gilpin and Whitley 1998: 3). Sorensen (2000) states that gender is not just women and men but "it is a result of the ways we live together and construct a universe around and gender as a basic structure of society is not stable" (Sorensen 2000: 7).

Nelson (1997) explains that certain roles, activities, or behaviour are assigned to particular people grouped together as a gender. In so doing, gender is related to sex, but is not the same thing. The construction of gender varies from one culture to another. Nelson goes on to state that ethnography "reveals many gender relationships as well as the varying negotiations between women and men within particular gender arrangements and their gendered contribution to the societies studied." It is reasoned that there are categories of male and female and "reinserting women as a category into the social and cultural equation fails to accomplish the full range of understanding that relational research may provide." Though what is male and female may be obvious in a cultural context, the same categories must not be extended to other cultures (Nelson 1997: 16-17).

Joyce and Claassen (1997) caution that gender should not be linked to labour organisation as shifts in labour organisation would render such linkage invalid. They then suggest that "as an alternative, gender may be about sexuality: the marking of individuals in ways that allows for sexual pairing within a society." This would clearly link sex differences to gender but the links may not be the same in the different cultures. This line of reasoning is strengthened when age is introduced as a variable in analysing gender and the implication of the instability of gender is considered. The consideration of variation in age then becomes crucial to understanding gender. "Elderly women may appear to be more like men than young women: children may fit into no adult gender. If children have separate gender, children may be related to their stage of sexuality and reproductive activity. When children's labour becomes essential to the work of society, their child-gender stage is foreshortened by adult-gendered expectations" (Joyce and Claassen 1997: 3-4).

Further, Joyce and Claassen argue that, "the idea that gender is a social category, an aspect of core personal identity, or any other fixed and immutable construct existing before the individual actor" lacks merit. Rather, gender would be "better understood as something that develops through particular practices engaged in by individual actors and evaluated differently in different cultures or cultural settings...gender is performance, marked by distinctive postures, gestures, and dress" (Joyce and Claassen 1997: 4).

The need to develop a separate sub-discipline of Gender Archaeology has been canvassed for in various ways. Claassen (1992) states that though the new archaeology argued that anything about past human life could be known if only we ask the right questions, instead of recovering whole past societies, archaeology has persistently de-gendered and de-cultured the past. She explains further that though archaeologists speak of the social organisation of past cultures yet we ignore gender. This act is seen as de-gendering or even de-peopling activities (Claassen 1992: 2).

Hays-Gilpin and Whitley (1998) queried archaeologists on the basis that we have for long "pursued an understanding of social and economic differences, especially the differences between elite and commoners, farmers and forages, and one ethnic group and its neighbours, but differences between men and women, and between adults and children, have been taken for granted" (Hays-Gilpin and Whitely 1998: 4-5).

The proponents of Gender Archaeology also recognise what we had noted earlier that what they are proposing had not been absent from the practice of archaeology. Conkey and Spector (1998) observed that "in spite of the absence of serious methodological or theoretical discourse" on the subject of gender, the archaeological literature is not silent on it. Gender structures and gender behaviour in past human life had been mentioned in archaeology but the problem is that "it is permeated with assumptions, assertions and statements of 'fact' about gender." This problem is traced to "the male-centred or androcentric bias in archaeology" which reflects the dependence upon ethnographic record in archaeological work. Archaeology is said to have inherited "the theoretical and methodological biases and problems of anthropology that generated the ethnographic interpretations and data." Also, the assertions and suggestions made by archaeologists about gender arrangements in the past are said to be often the "by-products of the consideration of other archaeological topics or are so implicit as to be excluded from the attempts of archaeologists to confirm and validate their inferences about past human life." The proponents of gender archaeology would rather want to see publications titled "'Methods for Examining Gender Through the Archaeological Record;" or "Gender Arrangements and Site Formation Processes;" or "Gender Arrangement and the Emergence of Food Production;" or more generally, "Gender Structures and Culture Change'" (Conkey and Spector 1998: 12-15).

Nelson (1997) states that "gendered archaeology considers both women and men, and any other culturally constructed genders… especially the relationships of women and men to the social, economic, political and ideological structures of particular societies." According to her, the goal of gender archaeology is not to 'make grand statements about woman's past, even when juxtaposed against man's past, but rather to elicit all the rich variety of experiences, behaviours and symbolic systems of social, economic and political arrangements of many kinds." She states that "gender is not a code word for women, and gendered archaeology is not another way of finding women in prehistory disguised with a more neutral and inclusive term," but adds that "finding women in the past who were overlooked and trivialised is a valid goal." She also raises the deeper questions about the categories of "women" and "men" to know if the characteristics attributed to women are the same everywhere. She further raises the question on how we can "tell if men's and women's roles are identical, similar, overlapping, or different in archaeological context." She expresses the view that "better and more accurate 'stories' about the past can be told when women and men, and perhaps additional genders where appropriate, are considered" (Nelson 1997: 15-20).

Sorensen (2000) re-echoes the views of Nelson when she states that the aim of gender archaeology is "to explore variations in prehistoric gender relations as well as the analysis of their generation and maintenance," and that the "important difference introduced with gender archaeology lies in the way women - and the relationship between women and men - are conceptualised: their recognition as subjects of study and the range of issues associated with this." We are also to see the active dynamic nature of gender and its role in the historical process to mean that gender construction and relations are issues of archaeological concern. Archaeologists are being requested to 'examine the factors that seem to influence the nature of relations between men and women, the circumstances in which women and men exert power and influence and the ways that gender arrangements affect or structure group responses to various conditions in the social or natural environment (Sorensen 2000: 5-7).

One thing becomes clear from the demands for gender archaeology and it is simply that we should endeavour to read from the archaeological data roles played by each of the constructed gender. It is also clear that what is actually at stake is identifying the roles of women in the past. But it is also recognised that where data did suggest gender arrangements in past studies had been mentioned. However, gender study in archaeology would need to contend with the number of genders identifiable in each society. Claassen (1992) drew our attention to this problem in the statement that "the question of how many genders there are in society is unanswerable from the perspective of material culture, spatial associations, or archaeological context." She further states that "we may have but one gender yet two sexes at some point in our history or multiple genders (Claassen 1992: 3).

THE TIV PEOPLE

The Tiv people live in the Benue valley of central Nigeria (Fig.9.1). They are the largest ethnic group in the Benue State of Nigeria. They are predominantly subsistence farmers and the Benue valley allows participation in both the grain-based economies to the north and the yam-based economies to the south. Farming activity is all year round (see Folorunso and Ogundele, 1993).

The Tiv can be said to be living on their farms though the need for additional farming land may send some away from their compounds to distant places

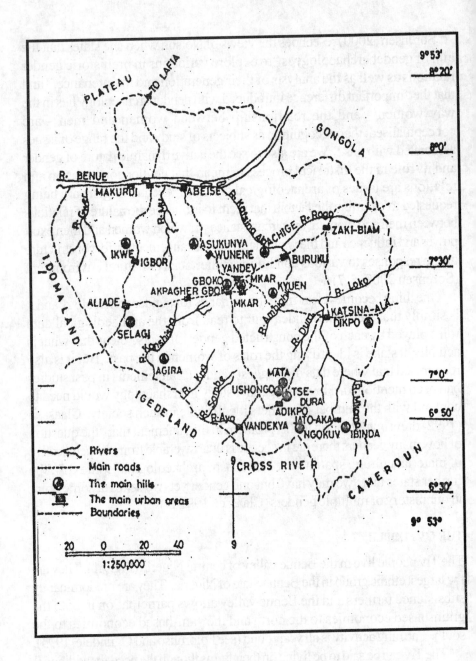

Figure 9.1: *Map of the Tiv area in the Benue Valley, Central Nigeria*

where they camp and return to their compounds afterwards. Both men and women clear the land, but men do the hoeing of mounds and ridges, as well as preparing the land for planting. While women harvest yams and the other root and vegetable crops, both sexes perform complementary tasks in the harvesting of grain crops. Both see themselves first and foremost as farmers, but differ in the practice of other crafts. Women are pottery makers while men are involved in smithing, weaving and woodwork. It has been estimated that men contribute only about 40% of farming labour (Briggs 1941).

Every married woman in Tiv-land owns a farm sufficient to cater for the needs of her immediate family. It is incumbent on the husband to provide such a farm and to perform, or oversee, the heavy work on it. Farm produce is kept in granaries or store-huts, which are in the exclusive preserve of the women. Women therefore play an important role in the subsistence activities in Tiv-land (Folorunso and Ogundele 1993).

If we bring the issue of gender into farming activities in Tiv-land, we are probably dealing with division of labour within this economic pursuit. Heavy work is reserved for the "able-bodied men," of course not all men, while "able-bodied women" do the harvesting, and both genders participate in clearing the land. We cannot overlook the labour of the male children in the assistance they offer to their mothers in weeding the farm because the women mostly do the weeding. Therefore there is the third gender, the "male child" in the farming activities. As we shall see in the section that follows, we can continue to define more and more genders.

The Tiv people live in circular huts of very thin mud walls. The walls are made of mud bricks or puddle mud, resting on a wide, raised base to keep out water. The roof, resting on the wall has an inverted conical shape. The huts are thatched with spear grass (*imperata* cylindrical). Huts are arranged in an oval or circular fashion, or perhaps an arc if the compound is very small (Folorunso 1998).

FINDS WITH ARCHAEOLOGICAL IMPLICATIONS FOR GENDER

House Structures and Gender

We were able to establish the importance of women in the Tiv compound when we started looking for data that would help in the understanding and interpretation of the archaeological settlements which present similar forms as the ethnographic settlements. Our archaeological study focused on the hilltop settlement in the same Benue valley. The work involved the use of ethno-archaeological methods (Folorunso 1989). In the process of collecting ethnographic data, it became obvious to us that the activities and roles of women might be more accessible for archaeological interpretation than those of men.

Our findings show that a compound may consist of one or more families, or even an extended family. When a compound consists of two or three families, the men of the families are usually full brothers (of the same father and mother) and compounds of their half brothers (of the same father but different mothers) may be situated some metres away. When a compound consists of a large extended family, the placing of the people is done on the genealogical relationship of adult males. A man lives closer to his full-brothers than he does to his half-brothers and closer to the latter than to his first cousins. The family of a man, which includes his wife and children, is usually represented on the ground by a sleeping hut, a kitchen and a store. If the man has more than one wife, usually each wife would have a separate sleeping hut, and a separate kitchen, while the man hardly has a separate hut of his own (Folorunso 1998).

Granaries where they exist or store huts are also associated with women, since each woman is provided with a farm for the subsistence needs of her dependants. It follows therefore that, with the exception of the reception hut which is centrally situated in a compound where it is present, all the units of the Tiv compound are associated with the women. This makes their presence highly visible while the presence of men is inferred from those of the women.

In terms of activities leaving traces when and if a compound is abandoned, it is also the activity of women associated with the kitchen that leaves tangible and visually recognisable traces. Of all the hut-types in the Tiv compound, the kitchen, which is the centre of female activity, would be the most visible in the archaeological context. The reception hut might be identified by its central location and posts on which the roof rests, but the kitchen is associated with features like a hearth which is usually located at the centre of the hut with a wooden drying platform over it. Grinding stones are also located in the kitchen. These are features that would have traces if the compound were to be abandoned.

Granaries, where they are present, are generally small in size and are located on the periphery of the compound. Where there are no granaries, there are store-huts which serve the same purpose and they form part of the woman's domain. The store or sleeping huts have no specific size or location and they are not associated with any feature that may leave a trace in the archaeological record.

If we were to identify individuals and estimate the number of persons in a compound from the structures, the woman becomes very visible while the man is at best anonymous. However, going by the definition of gender there are categories of women and men in the Tiv compound. If one applies what Ruth Whitehouse (2000) called 'becoming more female and male or less female or male', one would have to redefine what Tiv women would be. The Tiv women would be married women who fulfil the following conditions: living with their husbands, economically productive, and of sound body (not aged). We may call this category the "attached woman." This definition of Tiv women implies that there are several other categories of women in the Tiv compound. A second category would include those who are economically productive, of sound body but are unmarried or they have left their husbands to return to their fathers' compound. The concept of becoming more or less female applies here. A single lady in her father's compound is treated as a child; she is not entitled to a kitchen of her own but would use her mother's kitchen. She may have a separate sleeping hut where she can also make a fire and cook or even share a sleeping hut with others. In this case she is less female and becomes more female in her husband's compound. Therefore a lady may oscillate between these two categories, the "attached woman," and the "unattached woman" which would be the second category.

There is a third category of women consisting of the aged living with their husbands but they are no longer economically productive and they depend on their children for their subsistence. Such women share a sleeping hut with their husbands where they could make a fire to cook and keep warm. They may also use the kitchens of their daughters-in-laws; in essence such women have no separate kitchen of their own. In this category the woman becomes less female. We may call this category the "attached aged woman".

A fourth category would include widows who are economically productive and of sound body. They are not different from the first category of the "attached woman" because they still maintain all their rights in terms of facilities, viz. sleeping huts, kitchen and store room. The fifth and final category is made up of aged widows and we may call this category "unattached aged woman." Their situation may be a little different form that of the "attached aged." They are usually housed in the kitchen of their daughters-in-law where they sleep to keep warm and may also do some cooking.

For all the categories of women we have defined some may have parallels for the men genders. There is the "attached man" whose unit in the compound takes care of his wife. However, in the case of the category of "unattached man," there is variation in terms of how they are represented on the ground. There are bachelors who are entitled only to their sleeping huts. They may keep their agricultural produce in their mothers' granaries or store-huts and depend on their mothers' kitchen for feeding. In this sense they are less male but become more male when they get married and they would have to provide their wives with kitchens and granaries or store-huts. The story for a man whose wife had left him is different on the ground. He may abandon the kitchen or convert it into a sleeping hut or store hut. He still keeps the other units of huts but all the same he has become less male because he no longer needs a kitchen and he would depend on others for feeding. The "unattached man" are therefore less male and it is the taking of a wife that makes a man to become male.

The experience of the third category, the "attached aged man" is not different from that of the female counterpart. For male Tiv, the fourth category for the female, that is being widower, may not apply to productive and sound-bodied men because the Tiv are polygamous and a man may take another wife in the case of a death of his wife. However, the fifth category of "unattached aged woman" has its corollary for the males too. Aged widowers usually still keep their sleeping huts with a fireplace to keep warm just as with the "attached aged man" but they are sometimes relocated in the kitchen of their daughters-in-law.

Pottery and Gender

Pottery forms an important part of the activities of the Tiv and is still what vessels for food processing, cooking and storage are made of. Pottery is also the singule most important find in the archaeological context in Tiv-land as elsewhere in Africa from the later prehistoric period. Pottery in Tiv-land is in the exclusive hands of the women and they determine the forms, types and finishing we observe in the archaeological record. The female child learns the art of making pottery from its mother. It should however be added that while the male child is not consciously involved in or taught the craft of pottery, he assists the mother in some of the activities of pottery making, including digging and pounding of clay as well as firing the dry pots.

We can also examine gender issues in pottery production and use. Not all Tiv women are potters but all potters fall within specific categories of the female genders. A female child becomes an apprentice under her mother and she would practise the trade in her father's compound under her mother's control even after she had acquired competence as an independent producer. Her production forms part of that of her mother until she gets married and moves to her husband's compound where she becomes an independent producer. If she has cause to return to her father's compound later in life, she could continue to trade as an independent producer even if her mother is still active in the trade. The aged potters leave the trade to the young ones, as they become physically unfit. In essence, the potters are female who have learnt the trade from their mother and are physically fit. But we cannot overlook the participation and contribution of the young male child who in this case can be described as less male until he becomes an adolescent and disengages from this role of assisting the mother in pottery production. He then becomes more male as he leaves pottery production, which is considered to be the realm of the female gender.

We also established from the ethnographic study that the use of pottery also seems to be heavily weighted towards the women as pots are mainly found in the women domain in the Tiv compound. Therefore women tended to contribute more in terms of pottery in the formation of archaeological debris.

GENDER VISIBILITY IN THE ARCHAEOLOGICAL CONTEXT

Our main interest in the visibility of persons in the archaeological data was to project the ethnographic data into the archaeological realm. In other words what likely features are to survive if the compounds we studied were to be abandoned, disintegrated and buried? Can we reconstruct the presence of individuals from the remains of the huts that had been buried?

In response to the first question, the base and floor of the hut may be identifiable, as we have already seen in the archaeological settlements where the differences in dimension had been recorded. The hearth would be identified where a fire was burnt. Post-holes would be identified where posts were used. Grinding stones would be found where they were located. We can then answer the second question from the material evidence on the site. Materially, children are not taken into consideration in the plan of the Tiv compound and this makes their visibility very difficult. All adults, male and female, are taken into consideration in the plan of the Tiv compound, but they are not all materially visible.

The kitchen is an important feature to establish the presence of women while the presence of men can only be inferred from that of women. Therefore the men are not materially visible in the settlement plan. Not all women are visible, only those classified as "attached women" and the able bodied widows are visible because they own kitchens. No woman has more than one kitchen but could possess several granaries or store-huts. It follows therefore that the number of kitchens in a compound will correspond to the number of "attached women" there, and this has been confirmed in the ethnographic data. We therefore need to identify the kitchens. The presence of the hearth alone would not translate into a kitchen as we noted earlier that the elderly made a fire in their huts to keep warm and the "unattached women" may also have made a fire in their huts to cook. Kitchens are usually associated with a wooden drying platform over the fireplace at the centre but this is not a rule. Where the platforms existed, the post-holes would be preserved. The fireplace might not also be at the centre but every kitchen possessed one or more grinding stones.

We had used the presence of grinding stones to choose the remains of a hut on the archaeological site for excavation. The result was that at several levels we found grinding stones associated with a hearth, and we also found the post-holes of the wooden drying platform.

In the area of ethnographic pottery, there was nothing to suggest that men had special forms of pots associated with them. However, we recovered from our excavations a potsherd that had perforations on the shoulder, which the local people identified as a vessel in use no longer, but was used in the past for cooking ritual meat for the men. The man would prepare the meat, put it in the pot, cover it and hand it over to the woman for cooking. The perforations on the shoulder of the pot allowed steam to escape in the process of cooking.

CONCLUSION

It follows from our discussions that among the Tiv, the more female you become, the more visible you are in the archaeological record and the less female you become the less visible you are. Being more female is being "attached" to a husband, able bodied and productive, while a woman is less female if she is "unattached" to a husband or aged. The "unattached women" lose the right to possess a kitchen, which is a symbol of womanhood among the Tiv. Without a kitchen, the woman loses her visibility in the archaeological record.

REFERENCES

Briggs, G. (1941)
"Crop Yields and Food Requirements in Tiv Division, Benue Province, Nigeria." *Farm and Forest* 5: 15-20.
Claassen, C. (ed.) (1992)
"Exploring Gender Through Archaeology and the Study of Gender." In Schiffer, M.B. (ed.), *Advances in Archaeological Method and Theory* 7: 1-38. New York: Academic Press.
Claassen, C. and Joyce, R. (eds) (1997)
Women in Prehistory. Philadelphia: Pennysylvania University Press.
Conkey, M. & Spector, J. (1998)
"Archaeology and the Study of Gender." In Hays-Gilpin, K. and Whitley, D. (eds), *Reader in Gender Archaeology.* London: Routledge: 12-37.
Folorunso, C.A.(1989)
"Recherches sur la Continuite du Peuplement Tiv dans la Vallee de Katsina-Ala (basin de la Benue au Nigeria): Sondages sur le Site Ancien d'Ushongo et Ethnoarcheologie de l'Habitat Actuel." Unpublished *Ph.D.* Thesis, Universite Paris I, Sorbonne.
Folorunso, C.A.(1989)
"The Compound of the Tiv of Benue State of Nigeria: The Reality of Ethnoarchaeology." In Andah, B.W., Sowunmi, M.A., Okpoko, A.I. & Folorunso, C.A. (eds). *Africa: The Challenge of Archaeology*, 235-255. London: Heinemann Educational Books (Nigeria) Plc.

Folorunso, C.A. & Ogundele, S.O. (1993)
   "Agriculture and Settlement Among the Tiv of Nigeria: Some Ethnoarchaeological
   Observations," in Shaw,T., Sinclair, P., Andah,B & Okpoko A. (eds.), *The Archaeology of
   Africa*, 274-288. London : Rouledge.
Hays-Gilpin, K. & Whitley, D.S. (eds) (1988)
   Readers in Gender Archaeology, London: Routledge.
Joyce, E.A. & Claassen, C. (eds) (1977)
   Women in Prehistory: North America and Meso-America. Philadelphia, Univ. of Pennsylvania
   Press:
Nelson, S. (1997)
   Gender in Archaeology. London: Altamira Press.
Whitehouse, Ruth (2000)
   "Archaeology of Gender and Archaeology of Women: Is There a Need for Both?" Paper
   Presented at the Institute of Archaeology, London, Seminar Series, Autumn 2002: Women in
   Antiquity.

Essai de Typologie des Perles des Sites Archéologiques du Nord de Madagascar

Bako Rasoarifetra

Abstract: *Beads are important artefacts retrieved from archaeological investigations carried out in Madagascar since the beginning of the 20th century. Excavations in Northern Madagascar (especially on the western coast and part of the eastern coast) have provided thousands of beads (see for example Gaudebout & Vernier 1941; Vérin 1975; and Radimilahy 1998). Four archaeological sites have been chosen (Mahilaka, Vohémar, Antsoheribory and Andoka) where 33,000 beads have been studied.*

The present work is an attempt to establish a typology in time and in space, from the standardisation of characteristics of beads : material, shape, size and colour. Comparative study of the four collections showed that beads, such as pottery represent historical and archaeological time reference, thus a relative dating method.

INTRODUCTION

Les perles constituent une part importante des mobiliers mis au jour lors des fouilles archéologiques entreprises à Madagascar depuis le début du XXe siècle. La région Nord de Madagascar (plus particulièrement la côte ouest et une partie de la côte est), a livré des milliers de perles lors de ces travaux, entre autres ceux de Gaudebout & Vernier (1941), de Vérin (1975) et de Radimilahy (1998).

Cette étude sera limitée aux produits de quatre sites archéologiques importants dont Mahilaka (IXe-XVe siècle) sur la côte nord-ouest (C.G.N[1] 603.200/362.800), Vohémar (XIIIe-XVIe siècle) sur la côte nord-est (C.G.N 145.000/765.000), Antsoheribory (XVIIe-XVIIIe siècle) sur la côte nord-ouest (C.G.N 351.040/110.600) et enfin Andoka (XVIIIe-XIXe siècle) sur la côte nord-ouest (C.G.N 309.000/1107.070). Outre l'archéologie (Rasoarifetra 2000), la plupart de ces perles ont déjà fait l'objet d'études traitant essentiellement deux aspects, à savoir:

◆ Historique, car de temps immémorial et jusqu'à nos jours, la présence et la circulation des perles sont constantes et sont attestées par les traditions orales et par l'existence de différentes collections,
◆ Ethnographique, car on les trouve encore sur le marché avec les médicaments traditionnels et elles gardent toutes leurs valeurs magiques et protectrices.[2]

Du point de vue archéologique, les perles ont été découvertes dans des restes d'habitation et dans des tombeaux. Ceci nous a ramené vers la connaissance et la compréhension de l'installation humaine dans la région Nord de Madagascar car les dates d'occupation respective de ces sites s'étendent sur une dizaine de siècles. L'étude pourra ainsi nous aider à mieux connaître la civilisation de cette partie de l'île durant cette période et comprendre l'intensité des trafics commerciaux dans ce que Vérin (1972)[3] a dénommé "échelles anciennes du commerce" et leur civilisation matérielle, car en fait, les perles ont joué un rôle important dans les échanges commerciaux en tant qu'objets de troc. Au stade actuel de notre recherche, nous avons voulu présenter une esquisse de typologie de perles qui nous servira d'indication chronologique pour les travaux à venir.

METHODOLOGIE

Jusqu'ici les travaux relatifs aux perles se sont limités aux seuls descriptifs en indiquant la matière de fabrication, la couleur, la forme, les motifs et enfin le trou d'enfilage. Pour une meilleure exploitation des ces données, nous avons essayé d'établir une normalisation des études morphologiques des perles pour en dégager une typologie qui est loin d'être parfaite. Les caractéristiques

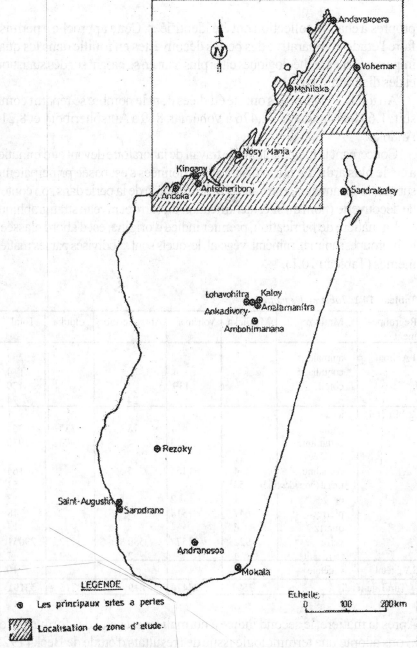

Fig. 10.1: *Les principaux sites a perles a Madagascar*

propres à chaque collection ont été identifiées. Cette approche a permis de faire l'étude comparative des perles découvertes en fouille dans les quatre importants sites archéologiques cités plus haut en se basant sur des statistiques et des diagrammes.

Au total, 33,111 perles ont été étudiées dont le nombre se répartit comme suit: 1,601 à Mahilaka, 22,476 à Vohémar, 819 à Antsoheribory et 8,216 à Andoka.

Concernant la méthodologie, le travail de laboratoire devant être minutieux a été le plus ardu. La normalisation des données s'est basée principalement sur quatre paramètres, entre autres la localisation de la perle dans son contexte de découverte (nom du site, identification du carré et niveau stratigraphique).

La matière de fabrication, premier indice d'origine, est d'abord classée en trois groupes: animal, minéral, végétal, lesquels sont subdivisés par les matières mêmes (Tableau 10.1).

Tableau 10.1: *Tableau des matières*

Regroupe-ment	Matière	Mahilaka	Vohémar	Antsoheribory	Andoka	Total
1 Animal	animale		1			1
	coquillage		4			4
	corail		139			139
	os			24		24
2 Minéral	agate	1				1
	argile			18	337	355
	céramique vitrifiée		23	4	1903	1930
	cornaline	4	155	5		164
	métal (non identifié)	53				53
	or	1	2			3
	pierre	647	514	185	2	1348
	quartz	6	4	1		11
	verre	922	21577	580	5972	29051
	terre cuite	4	2		1	7
3 Végétal	végétale	6	4			10
Total général		1591	22476	819	8215	33101

Après la matière, le second indice à normaliser est celui des formes.[4] Nous avons adopté une terminologie issue des résultats d'étude de Beck (1928)[5] reprise par Dubin (1988).[6] Sur la totalité des quatre collections, objet de notre étude, nous avons identifié 32 formes différentes lesquelles sont classées en trois catégories:

* La catégorie I comprenant les formes les plus simples qui correspondent à la forme brute des matières premières déjà travaillées ou réchauffées : annulaire, disque circulaire, sphérique aplatie, sphérique, tonnelet, cylindrique, tubulaire, etc;
* La catégorie II comprenant les formes travaillées à facettes, biconique, bitronconique, piriforme, losangique, tabulaire carrée, etc;
* Et la catégorie III avec les formes composées : segmentée, bitronconique concave, biconique concave, cannelée, à côtes de melon, etc.

Le tableau (Tableau 10.2) ci- après a permis de situer chaque collection dans cet ensemble de formes. Pour en faciliter la lecture, nous avons classé les différentes formes par liste alphabétique. Les formes dominantes sont représentées en pourcentage.

Tableau 10.2: *Tableau des différentes formes*

	Forme	Mahilaka	Vohémar	Antsoheribory	Andoka	Total
1	Annulaire	303 (18%)	21147 (94%)	369 (45%)	7817 (95%)	29636
2	biconique-hexagonale-facettée	3	1			4
3	biconique	3	1			4
4	biconique-convexe-courte	3				3
5	biconique-polygonale-facettée	1				1
6	bitronconique-convexe		1			1
7	bitronconique		1			1
8	conique	2				2
9	conique-convexe	1				1
10	conique-convexe-longue	1				1
11	cubique		1			1
12	cylindrique	349(50%)	179 (26%)	27 (4%)	130 (19%)	685
13	cylindrique-carrée	3	77			80
14	cylindrique-hexagonale-facettée		11			11
15	disque-circulaire	267(32%)	509(60%)		71 (8%)	847

Table 10.2: *Continue....*

Forme	Mahilaka	Vohémar	Antsoheribory	Andoka	Total
16 disque-conique-convexe	1				1
17 ellipsoïdale		6	1		7
18 lenticulaire	1				1
19 losangique	1	30			31
20 pentagonale		5			5
21 pendentif			1		1
22 roue dentée	1				1
23 piriforme			1		1
24 segmentée	1	5	1		7
25 Semi-circulaire	1	1			2
26 sphérique	64 (4%)	91	36		191
27 sphérique-aplatie	476 (46%)	301 (29%)	265 (25%)		1042
28 sphérique-hexagonale-facettée		19			19
29 sphérique-octogonale-facettée		27			27
30 tonnelet	72 (58%)	29 (29%)	21 (18%)	1	123
31 Tronconique-convexe-courte	1				1
32 tubulaire	46	34	26	267 (30%)	373
Total	**1601**	**22476**	**819**	**8215**	**33111**

En troisième indice, nous avons la taille qui est la plus variable et nécessite une classification de la grandeur du diamètre mesuré à l'aide d'un pied à coulisse électronique:

- Taille A, diamètre entre 1,2 mm à 2 mm: "perles minuscules"
- Taille B, diamètre entre 2 mm à 3,5 mm: "perles de petite taille "
- Taille C, diamètre entre 3,5 mm à 5mm: "perles de taille moyenne "
- Taille D, diamètre entre 5 mm à 9,9 mm: "perles de grande taille "
- Taille E, diamètre de plus de 10 mm: "perles de grosse taille ".

Les nombres donnés (Tableau 10.3) sont suivis d'un pourcentage par rapport à l'ensemble des quatre collections réunies.

La couleur constitue le quatrième indice qu'il a fallu normaliser quant à sa description. L'identification s'est basée sur une codification chiffrée utilisant les six couleurs- mères : le jaune (Y), l'orange (O), le magenta (M), le cyan

(C), le vert (G) et le noir (K), les nuances allant du plus foncé au plus clair. Cette échelle appelée Pantone Hexachrome Color Selector (Pantone Inc. 1963, 1965) identifie chaque couleur par un code suivant l'exemple: H10-8C:

- La lettre H identifiant l'Hexachrome;
- Un chiffre pour indiquer le numéro de la page;
- Un deuxième chiffre de 1 à 14 pour localiser la couleur ou la nuance;
- Les lettres C ou U pour indiquer la qualité de la couleur.

Tableau 10.3: *Tableau de répartition des collections suivant les différentes tailles*

Taille D:en mm	Mahilaka	Vohémar	Antsoheribory	Andoka	Total
A (1,2-2)	67 (5 %)	1272 (95 %)		2	1341
B (2-3,5)	804 (3 %)	20084 (68%)	149 (1 %)	8055 (28 %)	29092
C (3,5-5)	456 (24 %)	841 (44 %)	543 (28 %)	60 (4 %)	1898
D (5-9,9)	274 (38 %)	237 (32 %)	125 (18 %)	981(14 %)	734
E (+10)		42 (95 %)	2 (5 %)		44
Total	**1601**	**224746**	**819**	**8215**	**33111**

Par ce code, il est facile de reproduire les couleurs en se servant des formules indiquées en bas de chaque code couleur, ex : H10-8C est une couleur jaune dont la composition est Y=100, O=2, K=0 c'est-à-dire du jaune (100) + orange (2) + noir (0). La couleur de chaque perle a été ainsi identifiée selon cette norme permettant à chaque fois de regrouper les perles de même couleur-mère d'abord et les différentes nuances ensuite.

Plate 10.1: *Pelle cubique (de forme simple) de Vohemar comaline orange. Taille D Double perforation, typique de la periode XIIIe auXVIe siècle*

Plate 10.2: *Pelle de forme simple: spherique aplatie, spherique, tonnelet. Verre de couleur marron rouge indien). Opeque/brillant.*
Taille B Typique de la collection d'Antsoheribory

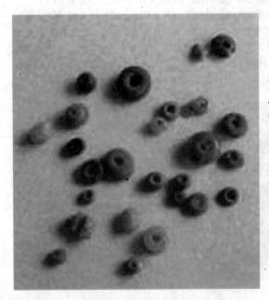

Plate 10. 3: *Pelle de forme simple: spherique, spherique aplatie,*
Taille A, B T
Couleurs: bleu, jaune, rouge indien. Verre opeque terne, verre translucide
Typique de l'occupaction 1b et IIa de Mahilaka.

Le diagramme suivant donne approximativement le nombre des perles pour chaque couleur-mère. Le tableau des nuances (Tableau 9.4) montre la variété des couleurs pour chaque collection. La couleur marron "rouge indien" (r.i.) est considérée comme une couleur-mère au même titre que les autres couleurs. Cette couleur est spécifique aux perles de fabrication indienne, les "perles de mousson," qui ont circulé dans l'Océan Indien.

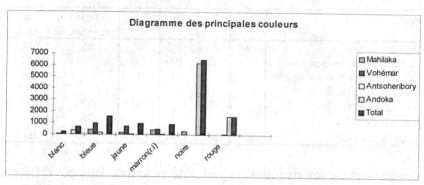

Fig 10.2: Diagramme des principales couleurs

Tableau 10.4: *Les nuances de couleur*

Couleur	Code	Mahilaka	Vohémar	Antsoheribory	Andoka
Bleu	H335-1C	19	7	20	5
Jaune	H30-1C	9	3	7	1
Marron, r.i	H635-1C	4	1	15	1
Noir	H670-1C	2	1	3	1
Orange	H150-1C	1	3	8	
Vert	H500-1C	10	4	14	4

ANALYSE DES DONNEES

L'étude des différentes données statistiques a rendu possible une esquisse de typologie des perles dans le temps et dans l'espace. Une première chronologie d'occupation humaine est avancée par Radimilahy (1998) dans ses résultats de fouille sur le site de Mahilaka qui s'étend sur 70 ha et est considéré comme la plus large cité swahili de la côte est de l'Afrique. Grâce à une fouille minutieuse, aux datations au Carbone 14 et en tenant compte de la chronologie des tessons de poterie d'importation découverts dans le même site, quatre niveaux d'occupation ont été déterminés:

- Occupation Ia située vers la fin du IXe au Xe siècle;
- Occupation Ib s'étalant du Xe au XIIe siècle;
- Occupation IIa allant du XIIIe au XIVe siècle;
- Occupation IIb allant du XIVe et bien plus au-delà du XVe siècle.

Le nombre de perles étudiées par occupation se répartit comme suit :

Secteur	Ia	Ib	IIa	IIb	Occupation non identifiée	Total Secteur
Intérieur du site	58		393	60	35	546
Partie nord vers les mangroves		22	109	463		594
Partie nord-ouest (limite du mur)	5		50	46		101
Vers l'intérieur des terres	2		8			10
Secteur du Fort				190	92	274
Intérieur du site					76	76
Total/Occupation	65	22	750	569	195	1601

Partant des caractéristiques de perles découvertes dans ces différentes occupations, nous avons pu établir une typologie selon les périodes. Pour le IXe au Xe siècle (première période d'occupation Ia de Mahilaka). Sur 65 perles étudiées (157 découvertes au total):

- Les matières premières dominantes sont la pierre (45) et le verre (20) ;
- Les formes sont généralement simples : disque-circulaire (20), sphérique-aplatie (13), cylindrique (12), annulaire (8) ;
- Les couleurs noire (29) et marron (rouge indien) (21) l'emportent sur le vert (5) et le bleu (6) ;
- Les tailles B et C sont les plus fréquentes: B (30), C (16). Neuf (9) perles ont la taille D.

Pour le Xe au XIIe siècle (période d'occupation Ib de Mahilaka). Nombre de perles étudiées: 22.

- Les matières premières restent le verre (17), la pierre (5) ;
- Les formes simples sont toujours en nombre : annulaire (16), disque-circulaire (3), cylindrique (3) et sphérique-aplatie (1) ;
- Les couleurs s'enrichissent : le marron 'rouge indien' (7) est toujours dominant avec le bleu qui apparaît (10), le vert est au nombre de 5, le noir

(2), le blanc ♦ la taille B (18) est la plus dominante, le reste revient à la taille C (3) et la taille D (1). En fait, les perles de cette période d'occupation sont caractérisées par des formes simples, de petite taille et de couleur à dominance marron 'rouge indien' et bleu.

Pour le XIIIe au XIVe siècle (troisième phase d'occupation IIa de Mahilaka). Sur les 750 perles étudiées:

♦ Les matières premières de fabrication se diversifient. Le verre est majoritaire (416). Il en est de même pour la pierre (326). On a pu identifier des perles en cornaline (3), en quartz (2), en végétal (2), et enfin en or (1);

♦ Les formes simples sont toujours nombreuses : shérique-aplatie (198), cylindrique (155), annulaire (147), disque-circulaire (137), sphérique (27). Les formes tubulaires (38) et en tonnelet (34) apparaissent. Cette phase est aussi caractérisée par l'apparition en petit nombre de formes composées comme le cylindrique-carré (3), le losange (1) le biconique-polygonal-facetté (1);

♦ Les couleurs marron 'rouge indien' (214) et bleu (163) restent dominantes. La couleur noire (153), le jaune (96) et le vert (72) prennent de l'importance en nombre. Le nombre de perles blanches augmente (34). De nouvelles couleurs apparaissent comme le gris (14), l'orange-cornaline (3) et le violet (1) ;

♦ Les tailles B (357), C (243) et D (110) sont les plus importantes en nombre. La taille A ne concerne qu'une quarantaine de perles.

Pour le XIVe au XVe siècle (quatrième phase d'occupation IIb de Mahilaka). Nombre de perles étudiées: 569

♦ Les matières premières sont toujours le verre (327) et la pierre (234) ; le quartz (4), la cornaline (3) et l'agate (1) sont très rares ; les perles en terre cuite sont au nombre de (2);

♦ Les formes simples : sphérique-aplatie (170), cylindrique (146), annulaire (116) se rencontrent en grande quantité. Toutefois on a moins de disque-circulaire (64), sphérique (33), tonnelet (25), tubulaire (3). Les formes composées telles le losangique (5), la roue dentée (1), le biconique-

convexe-court (1), le conique (1), le biconique (2), le biconique-hexagonal-facetté (1) sont en nombre infime;
- Les couleurs bleu (174) et marron 'rouge indien' (162) restent dominantes. Viennent ensuite le noir (84), le vert (60), le jaune (45), le blanc (28), le gris (13), le violet (1) et l'orange (1);
- Les tailles B (303), C (128) et D (117) restent en grand nombre. La taille minuscule A (59) varie très peu.

Au-delà du XVe siècle, période durant laquelle le site de Mahilaka a été abandonné, les références peuvent se porter sur les collections de Vohémar, d'Antsoheribory et d'Andoka, période correspondant au XVe - XIXe siècle.

Durant le XIIIe au XVIe siècle (correspondant aux phases d'occupation IIa et IIb de Mahilaka et à l'occupation du site de Vohémar), nous observons les mêmes caractéristiques:

- Les matières premières comme le verre (21 577) et la pierre (514) restent abondantes. Nous voyons apparaître d'autres matières comme la cornaline (155), beaucoup plus importante en nombre par rapport au site de Mahilaka durant l'occupation IIa, le quartz (4), le corail (139);
- Les formes simples sont dominantes : annulaire (21 147), disque-circulaire (509), sphérique-aplatie (301), cylindrique (179). Les formes travaillées à facettes (60) et composées sont en nombre grandissant (125).

Outre les petites perles polychromes (19 232), les couleurs dominantes retrouvées à Vohémar durant ces deux phases successives d'occupation sont : le bleu (961), le jaune (707), le marron 'rouge indien' (467), le vert (398) et le blanc (251).

La plus grande partie de la collection est de taille B (20 084). Les tailles A (1 272), C (839) et D (237) sont insignifiantes. La période du XIIIe au XVIe est caractérisée par les perles de grande taille. La collection de Vohémar se différencie des autres collections par l'existence de perles de taille E (+10 mm) au nombre de 42.

Les Caractéristiques des Perles du XVIIe au XIXe Siècle
Dans la collection d'Antsoheribory, le verre compte 580, la pierre 185. Les autres matières comme la cornaline (5), la céramique vitrifiée (4) et le quartz (1) sont rares. Pour le site d'Andoka, le nombre de perles en verre reste

important (5 828). L'apparition en nombre des perles en céramique vitrifiée (1 828) caractérise l'époque du XVIIIe au XIXe siècle. Les formes simples se perpétuent et restent majoritaires dans les deux collections (Antsoheribory et Andoka). Le bleu et le 'rouge indien' disparaissent pour donner la place au rouge et au.blanc. Les tailles B, C et D sont les plus nombreuses.

LA RÉPARTITION SPATIALE SELON LA TYPOLOGIE

L'étude comparative des quatre collections nous permet de voir l'évolution dans l'espace des types de perles qui ont circulé dans les comptoirs d'Islamisés de la région nord de Madagascar. Le tableau d'occupation des sites (Tableau 5) donne un reflet de la continuité d'occupation des échelles commerciales dans lesquelles les perles avaient circulé en tant que marchandises. Par ce même tableau, nous pouvons traduire la présence constante des perles. Si au tout début des premières arrivées des commerçants islamisés, les perles étaient encore rares (IXe siècle), leur présence s'intensifia à partir du XIIIe siècle.

Tableau 10.5: *Occupation des Sites*

Mahilaka											
Vohémar											
Antsoheribory											
Andoka											
Période d'occupation (siècle après -JC)	IX	X	XI	XII	XIII	XIV	XV	XVI	XVII	XVIII	XIX

Occupation de la Côte Ouest

Les différentes occupations traduites ici, en cascade, nous donnent tout d'abord l'image de la côte ouest beaucoup plus accessible aux implantations humaines. Il est évident que l'existence des baies et des îlots avait attiré les nouveaux venus à s'installer et les commerçants à faire leurs transactions. Les conditions d'implantation n'étaient pas aussi mauvaises, la description de l'auteur inconnu du bateau Frances en 1640 rapporte que:

> Il y a un endroit pratique pour faire provision d'eau, il y a de la pierre bonne à bâtir et
> pour faire de la chaux, il y a un grand fleuve d'eau douce où on peut faire le commerce du
> riz, des peaux de veau, de sucre brut, des moutons, des chèvres, des oranges, etc.[7]

Il semble exister une petite coupure d'installation vers le XVIe siècle sur la côte ouest, période correspondant aux razzias et aux essais d'implantation des Portugais à Madagascar, essais qui se traduisent en échec vers le milieu de ce même siècle.

S'il faut détailler la répartition spatiale des types de perles rencontrés sur cette côte ouest, il est intéressant tout d'abord de dégager le site de Mahilaka de l'ensemble de cet espace.

a) Mahilaka, sur 70 ha d'étendue présente un repère intéressant quant à l'évolution de l'occupation de l'espace. Les toutes premières installations sur le site se trouvaient au centre de l'ancienne ville (Occupation Ia), ensuite jusqu'au XIIe siècle la population s'était déplacée vers le nord-ouest, emplacement juxtaposant le mur de pierres qui délimite le site. A partir de l'Occupation II a, c'est-à-dire à partir du XIVe siècle, la population s'était éparpillée et avait occupé la totalité du site.

Les perles de verre sont abondantes, les caractéristiques sont apparentées au type " trade-wind beads " ou " perles de mousson " monochromes, opaques. On reconnaît la technique de verre étiré aux formes simples, aux couleurs dominantes 'rouge indien' et bleu.

Au stade actuel des résultats sur les trois autres sites de Vohémar, d'Antsoheribory et d'Andoka, il nous est encore impossible d'avancer la répartition géographique exacte de la population. Les données sont insuffisantes pour permettre de donner une estimation valable d'occupation.

b) Pour le cas d'Antsoheribory, le site aurait été habité par un millier de personnes vers la fin du XVIe siècle (Vérin 1975: 343). La superficie habitée ne dépassait guère les 4 ha, ce qui suppose une forte concentration de population. Les perles découvertes se trouvaient surtout dans les restes d'habitat localisé au centre de l'île. On retrouve les mêmes caractéristiques de perles en verre, en forte proportion, de forme simple et toujours de couleur à dominance rouge indien, bleu, un peu de vert, de rose et de jaune

c) Pour le site d'Andoka, Vérin (1975) le décrit comme étant une petite ville commerçante de 30 toits avec une population de 150 personnes vers le milieu du XIXe siècle. L'accès du comptoir était assez difficile pour les grands bateaux de sorte que seuls les boutres pouvaient y accéder. Cet handicap avait limité dans un sens les échanges et en même temps une occupation humaine importante. Une fouille archéologique exhaustive sur les emplacements des maisons aurait pu apporter beaucoup plus de renseignements sur la vie de ce comptoir. Toujours est-il que les perles de verre et les perles en céramique vitrifiée étaient répandues dans ce site. On remarque toutefois une nette différence entre les perles d'Andoka et celles des 2 sites cités plus haut. Si la forme reste en effet annulaire, cylindrique, et que les perles tubulaires commencent à prendre de l'importance en nombre, les couleurs changent; on ne trouve que du rouge, du noir, un peu de blanc, mais le bleu et le 'rouge indien' ont disparu.

Occupation de la Côte est

Contrairement à la zone ouest, nous n'avons qu'un seul site, jusqu'à l'heure actuelle, sur lequel nous disposons de matériels archéologiques suffisants. Lors d'une récente campagne de fouilles dans la région de Fénérive -Est[8] dans un ancien village qui s'appellerait "Lakaria," des perles en nombre infime ont été découvertes. Cet handicap ne nous permet pas de faire une comparaison quelconque avec d'autres sites, bien que quelques perles aient été découvertes dans les sites de Sandrakatsy (VIIe- Xe siècle), Nosy Mangabe (XIe -XVe siècle). Par ailleurs, les fouilles entreprises dans la région est ont été faites plus dans des tombeaux que dans des zones d'habitation.

Nous retenons toutefois l'importance du verre et de la pierre répandus dans le site de Vohémar. La diversité des matières utilisées pour la fabrication locale ou la transformation des perles (coquillage, corail, matière végétale, quartz, cornaline, or, cuivre et argent) supposent une florissante activité d'une population soucieuse de son aspect extérieur jusqu'à s'en parer dans les tombes. Les perles minuscules de différente couleur découvertes par milliers (19,232 unités) ne semblent avoir atteint ni le site d'Antsoheribory ni celui d'Andoka. Il en est de même pour les perles en cornaline. Elles sont spécifiques au site de Vohémar.

La présence des perles est un indicateur de l'implantation humaine dans la région du Nord. En faisant le rapport entre temps et espace d'occupation, on peut en déduire que le site de Mahilaka est la plus importante implantation dans cette partie de l'île.

EVOLUTION ET MODE

A partir de ces différentes caractéristiques nous pouvons suivre l'évolution et la mode des perles durant les diverses périodes. Le fait le plus marquant est la grande place qu'occupent les perles de mousson durant au moins dix siècles consécutifs. Il va de soi que les matières premières de fabrication restent le verre (opaque ou translucide) et la pierre dure. Mais à partir du début du XIXe siècle, les perles de moussons se font rares. Il est à noter que l'Inde, grande exportatrice de perles (en direction de l'Afrique occidentale et orientale, l'Egypte, le Moyen-Orient, l'Orient et l'Asie du Sud-Est), à la suite de la domination britannique, connaît un déclin économique vers le début du XIXe siècle. Elle est obligée d'importer de l'Europe 816 tonnes de perles en verre de 1879 à 1880 (Dubin 1988, p. 335). L'Europe, de son côté, grâce à des procédés plus modernes est arrivée à fabriquer des perles en plus grande quantité. Les formes et les couleurs sont les plus diversifiées. C'est ainsi que l'Europe supplante le marché indien en perles sur le plan international.

Les comptoirs du Nord de Madagascar ne sont pas en reste de l'évolution en matière de forme. En effet, à partir du XIVe siècle (occupation de Vohémar) jusqu'au XVIIe siècle (occupation d'Antsoheribory), les perles en tube apparaissent. Leur nombre augmente, atteignant aux XVIIe-XIXe siècles 271 dans la collection d'Andoka.

Du IXe siècle au XVIIIe siècle, les couleurs évoluent d'une manière plus ou moins constante dans les sites de Mahilaka, Vohémar et Antsoheribory où l'on observe 14 couleurs vives différentes, le bleu et le 'rouge indien' restant à la mode. Par contre, les couleurs retrouvées à Andoka sont à prédominance terne et peu diversifiées (75% de noire contre 18% de rouge et 2% de verte). Or, à partir du XIXe siècle, l'histoire des perles est marquée par la mode des perles polychromes et à motifs, de facture européenne.

Le comptoir d'Andoka ne semble pas être touché par cette vague. Pouvons-nous en déduire que les perles à motifs n'ont point intéressé la population du Nord en comparaison aux perles déversées sur le marché africain, perles dont la majorité est polychrome et à motifs divers?

CONCLUSION

Les perles, au même titre que la poterie, constituent un repère historique et un repère archéologique, en somme, un moyen de datation. Nous avons, en effet, présenté une esquisse de périodisation des perles en parlant des différentes phases d'occupation d'un site. Rappelons que les perles en verre "perles de mousson" sont de facture indienne et ont circulé à partir du début de notre ère et n'ont connu un déclin que vers le début du XIX e siècle. Elles sont opaques et monochromes. Les plus connues sont de couleur 'rouge indien'. Elles sont associées aux poteries sassano-islamiques et au sgraffiato du Golfe Persique.

Comme repère chronologique , résumons les différents types de perles selon les périodes indiquées:

+ *du IXe au Xe siècle:* perles en verre et en pierre, de forme simple, de taille moyenne, à couleur dominante 'rouge indien' et noir,
+ du Xe au XI e siècle : perles en verre supplantant la pierre en nombre, de forme simple, de taille moyenne, à couleur dominante 'rouge indien', et apparition de la couleur bleue,
+ *du XIIIe au XVe siècle*: prédominance de perles en verre, apparition des pierres semi-précieuses, de l'or, de perles tubulaires, en tonnelet et de forme composée, apparition aussi de perles de grande taille, de couleur diversifiée à majorité 'rouge indien' et bleu, avec du jaune, du vert et du noir,
+ *du XVe au XVIIe siècle*: mêmes caractéristiques que pour la période précédente mais apparition des perles en verre de taille minuscule de différentes couleurs (rouge, bleu, jaune, vert),
+ *du XVIIIe au XIXe siècle*: disparition des perles en pierre, apparition de la céramique vitrifiée, de taille moyenne ; disparition des perles de mousson, apparition en abondance de la couleur rouge et du blanc opaque.

Les perles en pierre comme la cornaline, l'agate, le calcédoine et le quartz, importées par les commerçants arabes ou islamisés sont contemporaines des poteries chinoises (céladon, bleu et blanc), du verre d'Iran, et colportées à partir du XVe siècle. Les perles en verre, d'imitation ou à motif, de facture européenne, sont des repères concernant l'emprise commerciale des Européens sur le continent africain à partir du XVIIe siècle. La présence des perles nous permet de retracer les contacts d'une population avec l'extérieur. Nous pouvons ainsi évaluer la durée d'une implantation humaine et même connaître l'évolution de sa culture. La répartition des perles constitue aussi une sorte de géographie d'occupation humaine avec laquelle on peut retracer le déplacement de certaines populations.

Ce travail, loin d'être parfait, n'a touché qu'une partie de notre vaste île, et les données actuellement avancées ne sont que partielles. L'esquisse de collection de référence présentée n'est que provisoire. Dans le futur, l'étude sera étendue aux collections des Hautes Terres centrales et à celles du Sud de Madagascar et à quelques spécimens des sites de la côte est. Ce travail devra retracer la route des perles, et par la même occasion, identifier les réseaux commerciaux qui auraient relié les côtes occidentales à l'intérieur des terres et nous donner des indications sur l'origine des populations qui auraient transité dans ces sites, leurs activités, la durée de leur implantation.

Un autre travail doit se faire sur les perles : l'étude comparative de nos collections archéologiques avec celles des pays de la côte orientale de l'Afrique et des Comores (Kilwa, Manda, Shanga, Pemba, Zanzibar, Bagamoyo, Dembeni). Les études antérieures semblent démontrer que nos perles sont les répliques exactes de celles en cornaline, en quartz, en agate, de celles en verre appelées "perles de mousson" ou encore des perles d'imitation originaires de l'Europe, découvertes sur la côte orientale de l'Afrique, le "couloir swahili" de Horton (1986). Ces perles sont les témoins de la participation active de Madagascar aux courants commerciaux initiés par les Islamisés d'une part et les Européens d'autre part. Jusqu'ici, nos études se sont basées uniquement sur des documents écrits (ouvrages de recherche et articles). Les résultats d'étude sur l'évolution de la recherche sur les perles font défaut à Madagascar. Nous ne devons pas être en reste de cette évolution. Il nous faudrait procéder aux analyses des perles (composition chimique, densité du verre, etc.) sur des échantillons de différentes périodes. Il faudrait aussi ouvrir la recherche vers l'extérieur, en étudiant les collections issues des fouilles des côtes orientales de l'Afrique, et de là, établir une nouvelle typologie propre à la région est-africaine. Ces informations nous permettraient de comprendre la part de l'Afrique dans les échanges commerciaux et culturels durant les temps anciens.

BIBLIOGRAPHIE

Beck, H. (1928)
"Classification and Nomenclature of Beads and Pendants," Oxford. Communicated to the Society of Antiquaries.

Bernard-Thierry, S. (1957)
"Inventaire des perles de fouille à Madagascar," Antananarivo. *Bulletin de l'Académie Malgache* 37: 101-141.

Gaudebout, P. & Vernier, E. (1941)
"Notes à la suite d'une enquête sur les objets en pierre de la région de Vohémar". *Bulletin de Madagascar* XXIV (Nouvelle série): 91-99.

Gaudebout, P. & Vernier, E. (1941)
"Notes sur une campagne de fouilles à Vohémar, Mission Rasikajy". *Bulletin de 'Académie Malgache* XXIV (Nouvelle Série): 100-114

Dubin, L.S. (1988)
Histoire des Perles de la Préhistoire à nos Jours, Paris : Editions Nathan. 364 p. Pantone Hexachrome Color Selector (1963, 1995), USA : New Jersey.

Radimilahy, C. (1998)
An Archaeological Investigation of an Early Town in Northwestern Madagascar, Uppsala, Sweden : *Studies in African Archaeology* 15.

Raharisoa, (1990-1991)
Ny Vakan'i Mahajanga : Andrana Monografika. Antananarivo: Ecole Normale Niveau III, Filière Lettres malgaches. Mémoire du CAPEN. 319 p. (Manuscrit).

Rasoarifetra, B. (2000)
"Contribution à L'étude des Perles des sites Archéologiques du 2ème millénaire AD Nord de Madagascar." Université d'Antananarivo: U.F.R d'Archéologie / Histoire de l'Art. Mémoire de maîtrise. 104 p. (Manuscript).

Van-der-Sleen, W.G. (1990)
"Observations sur les Perles de Madagascar et de l'Afrique Orientale", Antananarivo : Institut de Civilisations/Musée d'Art et Archéologie . Taloha 2 (réédition) : Arabes et Islamisés à Madagascar et dans l'Océan Indien : XI-XV.

Vérin, P. (1972)
"Histoire ancienne du Nord-ouest de Madagascar," Université de Madagascar : Musée d'Art et Archéologie. Taloha 5. 174 p.

Vérin, P. (1975)
Les Echelles anciennes du commerce sur les côtes Nord de Madagascar, Lille : Service de Reproduction des Thèses. 2 vol. 1028 p.

Endnotes

[1] Coordonnées Géographiques Nationales en kilomètres en projection Laborde.

[2] Plusieurs ouvrages ont traité les perles de Madagascar, entre autres, Gaudebout et Vernier (1941), Pages (1971), Raharijaona (1961), Van-der- Sleen (1990), Raharisoa (1990-1991), etc.

3   Les travaux de Pierre Vérin (1975) sur Les échelles anciennes du commerce sur les côtes
    Nord de Madagascar en deux volumes ont constitué les bases de données sur les découvertes
    en perles dans les sites d'Andoka et d'Antsoheribory.

4   Chittick (1974) a présenté une esquisse de chronologie des formes basée sur les découvertes
    en perles dans le site de Kilwa sur la côte est de l'Afrique. L'occupation de ce site aurait été
    antérieure à 1200 AD.

5   Beck est le premier chercheur qui s'est penché sur l'étude des perles et est devenu le guide
    spirituel des experts actuels. Son étude intitulée " Classification and Nomenclature of beads
    and pendants "(1928) donne les bases de description des perles.

6   Dubin (1988) dans son ouvrage sur Histoire des perles de la préhistoire à nos jours note une
    soixantaine de formes de perles.

7   Omaly sy Anio 9, (1982) : 62.

8   Campagne de sondages archéologiques en juillet 2001 initiée parle programme PCE (Projet
    côte Est) en collaboration avec l'Université de Toamasina et l'Institut de Civilisations/Musée
    d'Art et Archéologie de l'Univertité d'Antananarivo dans la région de Fénérive-Est.

INDEX